ARMADA

ARMADA

Patrick Williams

TEMPUS

First published 2000

PUBLISHED IN THE UNITED KINGDOM BY:

Tempus Publishing Ltd
The Mill, Brimscombe Port
Stroud, Gloucestershire GL5 2QG

PUBLISHED IN THE UNITED STATES OF AMERICA BY:

Tempus Publishing Inc.
2 Cumberland Street
Charleston, SC 29401
(Tel: 1-888-313-2665)

Tempus books are available in France, Germany and Belgium
from the following addresses:

Tempus Publishing Group	Tempus Publishing Group	Tempus Publishing Group
21 Avenue de la République	Gustav-Adolf-Straße 3	Place de L'Alma 4/5
37300 Joué-lès-Tours	99084 Erfurt	1200 Brussels
FRANCE	GERMANY	BELGIUM

British Library Cataloguing in Publication Data.
A catalogue record for this book is available from the British Library.

ISBN 0 7524 1778 9

Typesetting and origination by Tempus Publishing.
PRINTED AND BOUND IN GREAT BRITAIN.

For Dámaso de Lario,
friend, diplomat and historian

Contents

Acknowledgements

It is a pleasure to record my deep appreciation of the help given to me in the production of this book. Hugo O'Donnell was unstintingly generous in guiding me through many of the intricacies of the Armada campaign, and I am deeply in his debt and in that of his several colleagues in the *Museo Naval* in Madrid who patiently dealt with my questions. I am also much obliged to Janet Tamblin and Maureen Attrill of the Plymouth City Museum for their assistance in providing a number of important prints from Francis Drake's home at Buckland Abbey. Elizabeth Clifford, Jennifer Moore-Blunt, Helen Rawlings and Paul Wright patiently gave a great deal of their time, usually at short notice, in order to answer queries and provide resources. Very special thanks to Philip Williams, who made the book possible and to Andrew Graham-Brown, who did so much to stimulate my interest in the Armada. I am obliged to Jonathan Reeve, who kindly commissioned the book, and to Nicola Watson who saw it through the press with unfailing efficiency and cheerfulness.

The story of the Armada tells of a war between Spain and England, and this book is dedicated to Dámaso de Lario, who in five years of brilliant work as Cultural Attaché at the Embassy of Spain in the United Kingdom (1993-98) did so much to deepen and extend relations between Spanish and English historians.

List of illustrations

Reproduced by permission of: ★ Museo Naval, Madrid; ★★ Monesterio de San Lorenzo de El Escorial Patrimonio Nacional; † British Library; †† Plymouth City Museums and Art Gallery (Buckland Abbey)

List of maps

* Reproduced by permission of Museo Naval, Madrid

Prologue: Old Allies, New Enemies

The Monastery of San Lorenzo del Escorial, 20 January 1588

On 20 January 1588, Spain's Council of State met in King Philip II's great monastery-palace of the Escorial just outside Madrid to consider the acute crisis in Spain's relations with England. The council was the king's most prestigious advisory body and the councillors were his most senior advisers – men who were experienced at the highest levels of war and diplomacy. They considered the breakdown that had come about in the last decade or so in the relations between the two countries and discussed whether to advise the king to despatch the invasion fleet – 'the most happy Armada' – that he had long been preparing for use against England. The decision was so momentous that some councillors wanted to hold back from committing themselves to it, but all recognized that their advice to the king had to be unanimous and so those councillors who had doubts agreed, if reluctantly, to support their colleagues: the king should order his fleet to sail. Curiously, the councillors did not recommend that Spain should declare war on England; the Armada would attack a country with which Spain was nominally at peace. The councillors allowed themselves to hope that God would favour a cause that was manifestly His own.

But this was no crusade that the councillors were recommending; they justified their advice on defensive strategic grounds. In recent years the English had attacked Spain and her possessions across the face of Europe and around the globe. These attacks had been extraordinarily damaging: on the coasts of Spain and Portugal (which, since 1580, had been ruled by Philip); on the islands of the Azores, which played a key strategic role in the imperial communications of Spain and Portugal; on Spain's possessions of the Low Countries; on the territories in the Caribbean and the Americas that Spain knew as 'the Indies'; on the possessions of Spain in the Pacific Ocean. The councillors agreed that these attacks could no longer be endured, not least because the use of seapower enabled the English to choose their targets at will and without warning while forcing Spain to defend all of her many territories in order to defend any of them. English aggression was destabilizing the political system of the 'Spanish Monarchy' and threatening the prodigious wealth of the king of Spain. The most damaging of all the attacks had been on the very soil of Spain; in 1585 Francis Drake had plundered north-western

The Escorial.

Spain, and in 1587 he had launched a devastating attack upon Spanish shipping in the great harbour of Cadiz. No monarch, least of all the greatest king of his day, could endure such contumacy. Worse even than this, every year the English threatened the treasure fleet that brought to Spain the prodigious treasure of the Americas that lay at the heart of her political power. Again, it was Drake who led the way; in 1578 he had attacked Spanish shipping in the Pacific – something that had been so inconceivable that the Spanish had never even bothered to mount a defence system against the possibility of it happening. Indeed, so unerring was Drake's choice of targets that many Spaniards came to believe that he was possessed of infernal powers, and that he had a mirror which enabled him to see well beyond the horizons which limited the views of mortal men. But it was not just Drake – 'el Draque', the dragon – who was assaulting the power of Spain. In Europe, too, the English were undermining Philip's possessions: in 'the Low Countries', English military assistance fuelled the revolt against Spain that had been draining Spanish wealth since the mid-1560s; at the very end of 1585, Elizabeth of England had even dared to send a small army under the command of her personal favourite, Robert Dudley, Earl of Leicester, to help the rebels. It was this action in sending an army to assist the rebels against his majesty that finally persuaded Philip to send the Armada against Elizabeth. Philip believed that the rebellion in the Low Countries was only maintained by English assistance and that it would wither if that assistance was cut off. More than this, he believed that Spain had suffered too much from English aggression and had been too tolerant of it. His councillors of State now formally agreed

The Earl of Leicester (1532-88) landing at Flushing.

with him. The 'most happy fleet' would sail to protect Spain, her monarchy and her most important strategic and economic interests. Its rationale was defensive, and it would sail early in 1588.

The discussions in the Council of State, solemn as they were, were an elaborate sham for the councillors knew full well that the decision to send the fleet against England had been taken almost exactly two years ago, at the turn of 1585-86, and that it had been taken by the king himself. Philip had made his decision not in his capital city nor even in his great monastery but in the remote mountains of Aragon when he was on a state visit to the eastern kingdoms of Spain. The decision was made in solitary and intense isolation. It was made, too, in circumstances of profound personal importance, as Philip recovered from an illness which had all but killed him (in 1585 he had received the last rites of the Church). Central to Philip's decision to despatch the Armada against England was his recognition that time was running out for him, and that he had to resolve the problems in his relations with England in order to leave a secure inheritance for his son and heir. In a political sense, Philip understood that he had tolerated English aggression for too long, and in a personal sense he appreciated that he had now to resolve the problems that the English created for him while he still had the strength to do so.

When on 29 January 1586 Philip finally committed himself to sending his great fleet, he was determined that it would sail within months. He failed in this, and in 1587 he failed again. In 1588 he dared not fail again. Every statesman, soldier and sailor in Europe knew that he had prepared the fleet and they knew, indeed, virtually every one of its details – how many ships it consisted of, how many men were to sail on it, how many guns it had, how much ammunition, even how many cannonballs were loaded upon it, and so on. Central to Philip's decision to send the fleet had been the prescription that he himself had laid down that it should be prepared and sail in secret – that it should arrive unannounced and unexpected at the Straits of Dover, take on board the veteran troops of Spain's Army of Flanders and cross the Straits to land the soldiers in England. But by January 1588 even the pretence of secrecy was a thing of the distant past. Indeed, Philip himself had published a detailed inventory of his fleet, almost as if he needed to convince himself of its invincible greatness. Philip's failure to despatch the Armada was now beginning to damage his standing in Europe. Could he not send the fleet against the small island kingdom? Could he not quash English help to his rebels in the Low Countries? Was he powerless to stop English attacks on his own kingdoms of Spain and Portugal and his possessions in the Americas? The fleet had to sail, not just to stop English aggression but to protect the reputation of the most powerful king of his age. It had to sail, too, for rather more prosaic financial reasons. The fleet was costing 700,000 ducats a month to maintain, some 6% of Philip's free income. It was unthinkable that so much money could now be wasted. The question was not whether but *when* the fleet would sail. Across Europe, bookmakers had opened books on the success or failure of the 'Enterprise of England'.

In England, Elizabeth and her ministers knew full well what Philip was planning, although they were still divided by intense debate as to how best they should counter the threat. They, too, saw themselves fighting a defensive campaign: the power of Spain was too great, too near at hand and too threatening for England to tolerate. The longer Spain's power went unchecked, the greater it would become. England had to protect herself against the colossus of Europe. This was the more true because France – the only power that was strong enough and rich enough to counterbalance Spain in Europe – was incapable of action, torn apart by bitter civil and religious wars. Religious war was indeed embittering and complicating the politics of Europe. Elizabeth herself was threatened by a rebellion in Ireland; in 1580 the pope had mounted an invasion of Ireland that was supported by 600 Spanish soldiers and the fleet that transported the men was commanded by a Spanish admiral. Papal and Spanish interference sparked a revolt that had the most profound political, military and financial implications for England. Across the Narrow Seas, too, England had to defend herself; an enormous and seemingly invincible Spanish army was stationed in the Low Countries, twenty miles away from England; at any time it might be used to mount an invasion of England. Within England itself, a substantial Catholic minority was poised to rise in revolt when the Spanish fleet arrived. No one knew how many Catholics there were in England nor how loyal they would prove to be when the fleet arrived but Elizabeth had good reason to fear their loyalty; as recently as 1569 the north of England had seen a great armed revolt for the Old Church. That revolt had been crushed with stark brutality but it had been followed in 1570 by a papal bull which absolved English Catholics from their allegiance to Elizabeth and which made it legitimate in the eyes of the Church for them to plot the queen's death. Elizabeth had good reason not to take this lightly; year after year in the 1570s,

A late medieval sailing ship.

her brilliant spymaster, Sir Francis Walsingham, uncovered plots to have her murdered, some of them involving people who were close to her, and some of these plots were mounted with the active compliance of the king of Spain and his agents.

And yet in 1588, Philip of Spain and Elizabeth of England went to war with each other with the very deepest reluctance. Both had long resisted the clamour for war from strident voices at home. Both recognized that their countries had by long tradition been allies and that wars between them were the exception rather than the rule. Spain and England were normally joined together in alliance by their fear of France, the largest and richest country in western Europe. The two monarchs were united, too, by their innate conservatism. Both dreaded war for its expense and for its uncertainty. But in the summer of 1588 they were driven to war by a number of imperatives: political and strategic, financial and religious. In a personal sense, too, the mutual respect they had once held for each other had turned to hatred and loathing. Neither wanted war, but neither could withdraw from it. Elizabeth and Philip had met each other at least once, when Philip had become king-consort of England by marrying Elizabeth's half-sister Mary. Philip had sailed to England in a fleet of no fewer than 125 ships – about the same number as reached the Channel in 1588. The story of the time between the armadas of 1554 and 1588 is as interesting as the story of 'the Armada' itself, for it told of the process which drove Philip of Spain and Elizabeth of England to make war on each other against all their very deepest instincts.

1 England, Philip of Spain and the Daughters of Henry VIII

The Bay of Biscay and the Channel were placid in July 1554, and the armada of Prince Philip spent a comfortable week at sea before Philip himself disembarked at Southampton. The fleet sailed on to Portsmouth, where Philip's dazzling entourage of courtiers, churchmen, soldiers and administrators disembarked before riding in splendid procession to join him at Southampton. Many villagers in southern Hampshire cowered from them, fearing that they were an army of conquest. But this was a peaceful progress, and in Winchester cathedral, on the feast day of Spain's patron, St James (25 July), Philip and Mary Tudor, queen of England, took their vows of marriage. To acclamation, Philip became king-consort of England. It was the high-point of Anglo-Spanish friendship.[1]

Philip was twenty-seven years old in 1554. He was a reserved man, cold to those who did not know him, generous and loyal to those few who did. He had been born in 1527, the only son of the Emperor Charles V, the most powerful ruler of his day, and of his Portuguese wife Isabella. Philip revered his father but was somewhat intimidated by his charismatic and overwhelming personality. In truth he did not know him very well, for throughout his reign Charles was restlessly on the move, dealing with the problems of his enormous empire; by the time that Philip entered his twenties he had only spent the equivalent of six years in his father's company. He was brought up by his mother and loved her deeply; her death after childbirth in 1539, when he himself was twelve years old, was a lasting sadness to him.

Charles V ruled more of the earth than any European had ever done – the Holy Roman Empire, the residual states of the ancient duchy of Burgundy, and the Spanish crowns and their American possessions (see Chapter 2). He had decided as early as 1531 that he would break up his enormous territories, perhaps because he realized that they were too large for one man to rule. In that year he had vested the succession to the empire itself not in Philip but in his own brother Ferdinand. Philip resented his father's decision, for he desperately wanted to enjoy the unique prestige that the imperial title conferred on its holder. But he had to accept it.[2]

Indeed, the same was true of his marriage to Mary Tudor. Philip did not want to marry the queen of England but filial and political loyalty compelled him to proceed with the match. He had already been married once, to his Portuguese cousin María, but she had died after childbirth in 1545. The son who cost

Medals of King Philip II (1527-98) and Queen Mary I (1516-58) of England.

María her life was named Carlos after his grandfather, and already by 1554 there were grave concerns about his psychological and physical development. Philip was deeply committed to uniting the royal houses of Spain and Portugal and had wanted to re-marry within the Portuguese royal house. But Charles V insisted on the English marriage and stipulated that any children of Mary and Philip would inherit England and the Low Countries. Moreover, it was unlikely that Don Carlos would be capable of begetting heirs, and if he failed to do so the children of Mary and Philip would also inherit the Spanish thrones. Implicit, therefore, in the marriage of Mary and Philip was the construction of a fabulous dynastic alliance between Spain, England and the Low Countries. The first part of this alliance was already in place: on his first journey abroad (1548-1551), Philip had been sworn in as heir to each of the provinces of the Low Countries, and now on his second journey he brought England into Charles V's grand design.

Implicit, too, in the marriage was the imminence of Charles V's abdication of power. Still only fifty-four years of age, Charles was worn out by the exertions of more than thirty years of ceaseless endeavour, and the marriage of his son with the queen of England was a key part – the central part, indeed – of the arrangements that would facilitate his abdication. It was his intention to relinquish power so that he could spend his last years in a monastery praying for his eternal salvation.

Charles's grand design of a union between Spain, England and the Low Countries depended upon Mary being able to have a child. Yet Mary was already thirty-seven years of age in 1554, and was known to have had a history of gynaecological troubles. Philip was certainly aware of this and when he met Mary for the first time all his worst fears about her were realized; his closest adviser, Ruy Gómez de Silva, wrote back to Spain that Mary was 'old and flabby'. Soon, Ruy Gómez was musing on the sexual difficulties of the

Charles V (1500-58) and his brother Ferdinand (1503-64).

newlyweds. His information could only have come from his close friend and sovereign.[3]

Mary Tudor was the daughter of Henry VIII and Katharine of Aragon (herself the daughter of Ferdinand and Isabella of Spain). She was born in 1516 and was the only one of Katharine's six children to survive the first weeks of childhood.[4] As Katharine grew older, Henry VIII became ever more concerned at the prospect of leaving his kingdom to his daughter. There was no legal impediment to a woman succeeding to the throne of England, but it was generally considered impractical to expect a woman to rule by herself while in taking a husband she would run the risk of being dominated by him. Received opinion held that female monarchy was, by definition, weak monarchy. Of course, this was a theory – or prejudice – as yet untested: no woman had ever sat on the throne of England as a queen-regnant in her own right. Henry therefore determined that, since it was imperative that he have a male heir, he had to end his marriage to Katharine. A justification for annulling his marriage was at hand; Katharine had been married to Henry's elder brother Arthur in 1501, and after Arthur's death in 1502 the papacy agreed to grant an annulment of the marriage on the grounds that it had never been consummated and so was canonically invalid. Henry duly married Katharine in 1509. By the later 1520s the king was becoming anxious that the failure of his wife to produce a male child was a divine punishment for his having married his brother's widow. As

Charles V seated, c.1547.

a keen theologian he reflected ruefully upon the biblical 'Curse of Leviticus' which forbade a man to take his brother's widow as wife. But annulments were no longer as easily obtained as they had been twenty years before; the challenge to the authority of the Catholic Church by the Protestant reformers of the 1520s forced Rome to stand much more strictly on the implementation of its doctrines and practices than it had recently done. Moreover, the papacy could hardly grant an annulment against the wishes of Charles V, who was the nephew of Katharine of Aragon and had the power to ensure that she was not humiliated in this fashion. Henry could not force either pope or emperor to change their mind, and so he broke with both of them and established a Protestant Church of England. He then married his mistress, Anne Boleyn, in the hope that she would present him with a son. But on 7 September 1533 Anne gave birth to a daughter. The child was named Elizabeth.

Henry forgave Anne her failure to present him with a son but when, in January 1536, she had a miscarriage of a boy, he decided once again that he had to divorce. But Anne could not be confined to a convent as Katharine had been. Instead she was despatched to the Tower of London on a charge of adultery and on 19 May 1536 was beheaded. Henry married again – Anne Seymour, another lady of the court – and his third marriage at last brought him a son, Edward, in October 1537. Anne Seymour's triumph was dearly bought, for she died a few days later. Henry married three more times but he had no more legitimate children and when he made his final dispositions he was forced to re-legitimize his two daughters so that they could stand in line of succession in case Edward failed to produce an heir. He died in 1547 and was succeeded by his son.

Edward VI's reign (1547-1553) was as important as it was brief, for the ministers who controlled him pushed ahead with a radical Protestant settlement. He died in 1553, still a child and unmarried. Henry VIII's worst fears now materialized: the succession passed to his two daughters. As the elder of them, Mary became queen.

Mary Tudor had refused to compromise her religious beliefs under her father and her brother and it was evident in 1553 that she intended to bring England back to the Roman Catholic faith. The marriage with Philip was central to Mary's commitment to re-catholicize England, for the strength of Spain would help guarantee the settlement that she intended to bring about. Unfortunately, it was clear from the outset that many opposed the marriage on religious or political grounds. Indeed, Philip's departure for England had to be postponed while Mary dealt with a rebellion in 1554 led by Sir Thomas Wyatt. Mary dealt efficiently with the revolt and Wyatt went to the block. So, too, did Lady Jane Grey, involved as a pawn in the rebellion. Mary suspected that Elizabeth had played some part in Wyatt's uprising and summoned her to London to account for herself. Elizabeth was brought to the capital by her great-uncle, Charles Howard, Lord Effingham, and was held briefly in the Tower of London in the spring of 1554. But nothing could be proved and Mary chose not to execute her.[5]

Necklace of the Order of the Golden Fleece.

In November 1554, England was formally reconciled to the Roman Catholic Church after twenty years of schism. In years to come Philip remembered the return of England to the Roman Catholic faith as one of the great achievements of his life. Yet this was a temporary accomplishment. England's status as a Catholic country depended upon the queen producing an heir. There seemed genuine cause for optimism when, in the spring of 1555, it was announced that Mary was pregnant. Yet this triumph soon revealed itself to be tragedy. Desperate to conceive, she had deluded herself that she was with child, possibly even mistaking a developing cancer of the womb for a pregnancy. During the summer of 1555 it slowly dawned on everyone – last of all, on the queen herself – that she was not pregnant. It seemed unlikely that she would ever produce an heir. With each month it became more evident that the succession to the English throne would pass to Elizabeth.[6]

Philip II (1527-98) as a young king.

The abdications of Charles V had waited (among other things) on the delivery of the queen of England and when it became evident that Mary was not going to produce the child whose birth would round out his grand design, Charles decided to proceed with the handover of power to his son. Philip left England in September 1555, and in October in Brussels, Charles placed the

*Philip II (1527-98),
Antonio Moro: 'The
San Quentin Portrait'.*

Don Carlos (1545-68).

Low Countries in his hands. In January 1556 the old warrior relinquished the Spanish lands to his son.[7] Charles left for Spain to retire into the monastery of Yuste in Extremadura.

In all probability Philip would not have returned to England by choice but diplomatic conditions forced his hand. Mary had agreed that England would go to war with France in support of the house of Habsburg and Philip needed to raise troops in England. On 5 July 1557, he left England for the last time, taking with him 7,221 English soldiers for his army in France.[8] The Englishmen played an important part in the great battle of St Quentin just outside Paris which was fought on St Lawrence's Day, 10 October 1557. It was a singular achievement on the part of Mary and Philip to make a successful war against the French unpopular in England, but the crass way in which they used English resources (and men) for a war in which England had no real interest managed to do just that. Worse followed: in January 1558, the French conquered Calais, the last redoubt of the old Anglo-Angevin empire in France. The Anglo-

Mary Stuart, Queen of Scots (1542-87).

Spanish marriage had brought about a national humiliation at the hands of the French. Mary's strength gave way under the escalating disasters and she died on 17 November 1558. Philip admitted to feeling 'a reasonable regret' for his wife's death. He looked to preserve the English alliance; he let it be known to the new queen that he was prepared to marry her.[9]

The diplomatic, confessional and political circumstances surrounding Elizabeth's first years as queen of England were deeply complex. Essentially, three factors shaped the course of events. First, on the diplomatic level it was imperative for both England and Spain to resist the claims to the throne of England advanced by Mary, queen of Scotland. This was because of Mary's proximity to the French court. Second – and most importantly – it was believed that Elizabeth was certain to marry. Third, these points were worked out in the unique circumstances of the religious 'settlement' imposed upon the English church by Elizabeth in 1558-9.

The threat posed by Mary Queen of Scots should be dealt with first. Philip was determined to retain the English alliance, and this was inspired by more than simply the need to retain English military support, important though that was. He was earnest in his pursuit of Elizabeth's hand during the first months of her reign; she mischievously encouraged his overtures before rejecting them at the turn of 1558-9. If Elizabeth died without heirs, it was probable that the succession would pass to Mary Stuart, queen of Scotland, and her accession to the English throne would join France, Scotland and England into a power bloc that would rival the strength of the House of Habsburg itself. Philip was determined to prevent that from happening and so throughout the early years of her reign he consistently supported and protected Elizabeth of England in order to baulk Mary Stuart.

Mary Stuart's claim on the English throne was a strong one; she was the granddaughter of Henry VIII's elder sister Margaret by her marriage with James IV of Scotland. She had become queen of Scotland at the age of one week in 1542 and in 1548 was sent to be educated at the French court while her mother, Mary Guise, ruled Scotland in her stead. Mary Stuart grew to adulthood, therefore, as a francophile and it was curiously suggestive of the direction that her life had taken that while she was fluent in French she could not even speak the language of her native land.

Elizabeth could make little progress at home while England remained at war and it was a happy chance that within months of her accession the two great powers recognized that they needed peace with each other. The Habsburg-Valois wars were brought to an end by the Treaty of Cateau-Cambrésis in April 1559. The settlement confirmed Spanish pre-eminence in Italy. It was agreed that Philip himself would seal the new friendship with France by marrying Elizabeth, the daughter of the French king, Henry II. France was confirmed in its ownership of Calais, although Elizabeth had the proviso inserted in the treaty that this would be reviewed after seven years. This saved English face, but more importantly it saved English money, for it was very expensive to maintain the garrison, and in reality Elizabeth was well rid of Calais – although she would never bring herself to acknowledge the fact.

However, exactly as western Europe paused for breath after its great wars the settlement reached at Cateau-Cambrésis was thrown into jeopardy by the death of Henry II, killed in a jousting accident at a tournament to celebrate the treaty (10 July 1559). His death brought Francis II to the throne. The new king was a minor and his mother, Catherine de' Medici, governed for him. But others fought Catherine for control over the new king. Francis was married to Mary Queen of Scots, and she was a daughter of the house of Guise, the most powerful noble clan in France, a family distinguished by its ambition and its aggressive Catholicism. The new pre-eminence of the Guise family created fear and resentment among their noble rivals, notably the Montmorency and Bourbon families. France headed for baronial war for control of the young king.[10]

Few expected much of Elizabeth in 1558. True, she was a highly educated young woman who spoke a range of languages ancient and modern: Greek, Latin, French, Italian and Spanish. She possessed the accomplishments

Medals of Catherine de' Medici (1519-89) and her sons, all of whom became kings of France.

expected of a young royal woman but these were hardly the qualities needed to tame and rule a land that desperately needed strong leadership.[11] But beneath the somewhat delicate appearance, Elizabeth had the fiery temper and iron resolve of her father. She had, above all else, an unbreakable determination to survive as queen, and experience had taught her well the political arts. She had learned how to disguise her intentions, how to give political messages without committing herself. She had accommodated herself to Catholicism under her sister, attending mass and receiving communion, but yet allowing people to doubt the sincerity of her attachment to the old religion. In many respects, it would have been difficult for Elizabeth to be anything else but a Protestant – her very conception had, after all, marked the break with Rome. She remained always loyal to both her parents, and her Protestantism was an expression of this loyalty.[12] She did not, as she famously put it, want to make windows into men's souls and she found the idea of religious crusades repugnant. Her politics were highly practical, rooted in her deep reverence for all monarchy – and most especially, of course, for her own. She demanded loyalty and service and was prepared to turn a blind eye to men's religious practices as long as they did not compromise or threaten her political survival. But if they did, she was every bit as merciless as her father. And she understood how financial resources defined monarchy's capacity. Unlike her father (but very much like her grandfather, Henry VII) Elizabeth was parsimonious. Taxes were hard to collect and Elizabeth did not fritter them away. Her vacillation in international affairs in part arose from a singular refusal to spend money unless she absolutely had to do so. She was determined from the very beginning of her reign to make her own decisions on major matters, especially in foreign and financial policy. She would take advice from her ministers (and play them off against each other) but she alone would decide on policy.

Of course, all of this came to light only with the passage of time. Her independence of action was first made manifest in her steadfast refusal to do what everyone expected. Queens married: it remained as much a rule of political life in the 1550s as it had been in the 1530s. But Elizabeth understood that if she married she would almost certainly lose her independence to her husband. Marriage to one of her foreign suitors would almost certainly entail involvement in wars brought about by her husband's dynastic interest – as had been the case with Mary. Moreover, it would almost certainly lead to a readjustment – and probably a drastic one – of doctrine and status of the Church of England. Nor could she retain her independence at home if she married a subject, for that would aggravate rather than lessen the growth of factions that was so much a part of court life.

It may well be, however, that Elizabeth had toyed with the idea of marrying a subject at the beginning of the reign, for she had a deep attachment to Robert Dudley, son of the late duke of Northumberland. He was a dashing, glamorous figure but unfortunately he was already married. This changed when, in September 1560, Dudley's wife died in circumstances which were deeply mysterious. Elizabeth accepted that the risk of scandal was too great. She could never marry Dudley, although she remained deeply fond of him for nearly thirty years. Instead she made a courtier of him so that he would remain at her side as a man of standing and substance; in October 1562 Elizabeth appointed him a privy councillor and in September 1564 raised him to the earldom of Leicester.[13]

It is far from clear when Elizabeth decided that she would not marry – perhaps she had done so by the mid-1560s – and she received suitors for the next quarter of a century or more. The more astute observers came to suspect that these courtships were designed to give the impression that she intended to marry and secure the succession. Her attitude caused deep distress to her advisers and to parliament, most notably when in October 1562 she almost died as a result of smallpox and the security of the realm manifestly hung by the most slender of threads. But as her ministers and her parliament begged her to marry – and sometimes tried to bully her into doing so – Elizabeth held her counsel. No one else seems to have even considered the possibility that a single woman on a throne might choose to retain all her options by not marrying. But Elizabeth's bottomless prevarication about marrying may well have been an early sign – for those who were able to read it – of her unique political brilliance. She would survive by breaking the rules of politics and by making up her own as she went along.

There was another element in Elizabeth's decision not to marry. The psychological tensions within her that must have come about as a result of her father having her mother executed for treason (and illegitimizing her) may well have been aggravated by some unpleasant experiences after Henry VIII's death, for as she entered adolescence, Elizabeth was subject to the abusive attentions of a powerful man. Henry VIII's last wife, Katherine Parr, had been kind to

Elizabeth and when, only three months after Henry's death, Katherine married Sir Thomas Seymour, she allowed Elizabeth to live with her. Seymour took to visiting Elizabeth (who was now fourteen years of age) in her bedroom in the mornings. What, if anything, happened is not known but Seymour's behaviour toward the princess was at the very least indecorous and at worst it was abusive. One day in a frolic in the garden he tore Elizabeth's dress to pieces while Katherine restrained her. Why Katherine should have involved herself can only be a matter of conjecture, but even she drew the line when some time later she came across her husband cuddling the princess; Elizabeth was sent away. The effects of these experiences on a young woman may be imagined: did they increase her wariness of men, and teach her about the dangers of commitment?[14]

Whatever Elizabeth's thoughts about marriage in 1558, she was wise enough to know that she needed political support and guidance and astute enough to make the finest appointment of her reign at the very beginning of it, when she named William Cecil as her Secretary of State. Elizabeth had known Cecil since 1550 and expressed her opinion of him when she named him to his new position: 'this judgement I have of you that you will not be corrupted by any manner of gift and that you will be faithful to the state'. No English sovereign ever trusted a minister for as long as Elizabeth trusted Cecil. In February 1571 she raised him to the baronage as Lord Burghley and in June 1572 appointed him as her Lord Treasurer. Burghley repaid her with unstinting loyalty and devoted hard work until he died in 1598. Elizabeth had found the anchor in her life.[15]

In 1559 Elizabeth pushed through the Acts of Supremacy and Uniformity which re-established the king or queen of England as head of a Protestant Church of England. Until relatively recently, these acts were seen as a triumphant 'settlement' of the confessional problem. According to this view, England was already a Protestant country in 1558. Elizabeth's return of the realm to Protestantism was a manifestation of the national will and a rejection of all things popish and Spanish – that is to say of Mary, her husband, the catastrophic intervention in France and the burning of Protestants at Smithfield. All of this has been seriously modified of late. It is now clear that the great majority of Elizabeth's subjects adhered to the old religion. Indeed, in many respects, so too did Elizabeth herself. She maintained candles and a crucifix in the royal chapel, and repeatedly replaced them when Protestant iconoclasts removed or defaced them. These were precursors of more serious problems. It is also important to stress that the circumstances surrounding the birth of the Elizabethan English church had fused political and confessional loyalty. The consequences of this were to become evident only after Elizabeth's excommunication (1570), which in theory at least freed her Catholic subjects from their duty of obedience to their sovereign. Jesuit missionaries to England would be brought to trial and condemned in secular, not religious, courts. As the Roman church intensified its campaign against Elizabeth and her church, it

Sir William Cecil, Lord Burghley (1520-98).

became increasingly difficult for English Catholics to reconcile their loyalty to both Rome and Elizabeth.[16]

Philip found himself both drawn to Elizabeth and repelled by her. While attempting to protect her from excommunication, he was also profoundly conscious that a Protestant England would eventually come into conflict with a Catholic Spain. This was especially true considering that both he and Elizabeth presided over expanding maritime powers. In the early modern world, pirates operated under the cloak of religion; English adventurers would pose a threat to Spain's enormous and as yet undefended empire in the New World.

Historians have striven to determine the extent to which Philip was conscious of the danger of forcing Elizabeth and her subjects into a defiantly Protestant stance. As king-consort to Mary, he may have sought to moderate the executions at Smithfield; there was an acute danger' in appearing a manipulative intruder. He probably shared the assumption that Elizabeth would marry a Catholic prince, and in these circumstances it made no sense to make an enemy of Elizabeth unless he had to: this was, perhaps, the reason why Philip never formally declared war against England. Paradoxically, by waging war on Elizabeth in the 1580s Philip identified the Roman Catholic religion in the eyes of Englishmen with an aggressive and tyrannical foreign power. In doing so, he played into the hands of Protestant polemicists such as John Foxe (1516-1587), who sought to portray the king of Spain as one of the dark forces behind the Marian suppression of Protestantism. In short, Philip of Spain and his invincible armada were to become one of the founding stones of English nationalism.

2 The Spanish Monarchy

The death of Henry II in 1559 and the turbulence into which it plunged France made possible what has become known as 'The Age of Philip II'. For over thirty years France was consumed by internal strife and unable to play her natural role in Europe as a counterbalance to Spain. Spanish power therefore developed largely unchecked. Aside from the eclipse of his major European rival, Philip II's hegemony was the consequence of extraordinary wealth. As the reign developed, his sources of income expanded. The flood of silver from the New World reached a torrent around the middle of the second half of the sixteenth century. By 1580, Philip II's Spain had become the first modern superpower.[1]

This rise to pre-eminence was the more astonishing because Spain had only been created at the end of the fifteenth century. Two remarkable monarchs, Isabella of Castile (1474-1504) and Ferdinand of Aragon (1479-1516), had joined their kingdoms together but without formally merging them into a new state. The 'Union of the Crowns' led to the creation of a new power in Europe; after Ferdinand and Isabella had completed the centuries-long *reconquista* of Spain from the African Moors by conquering the kingdom of Granada in 1492 (and thus earning themselves the title of the 'Catholic Kings'), they turned their attention and energies to external conquest. In 1504 they conquered the kingdom of Naples and in 1512 added Navarre to the Union. Spain – or, more correctly, 'the Spanish Monarchy' – became a rival to France in European affairs. Indeed, by the early years of the sixteenth century, Spain was threatening to leave all her Christian rivals in her shadow, for she was beginning to develop an empire across the Atlantic in the new world of the Americas.

The kingdom of Castile, which had a population of about 4,500,000 in the 1520s, was by far the more powerful of the two states of the Union, having three-quarters of the land and two-thirds of the people of the Iberian peninsula. However, much of Castile was barren and allowed for comparatively little arable farming. On the poor soil of northern Castile ('Old Castile'), sheep-rearing predominated as the basic economic activity, and Castilian wool was sold in large quantities in northern Europe, notably in the Low Countries. It was normally transported there in ships operating out of the three Basque provinces of Guipúzcoa, Vizcaya and Alava, provinces which were not formally tied to Castile but which were in practice controlled by her. These three regions were sparsely populated; together with Navarre they had a population of only about 300,000 in the 1520s. However their people were expert in the sea and its crafts of shipbuilding, navigation and fishing.[2] The northern sailors

Diego Homem, Map of Spain, 1563.

were familiar with the treacherous waters of the Bay of Biscay and they were regular visitors to the Channel. Indeed, Basque fishermen often ventured deep into the North Atlantic.

The eastern states of Spain formed a separate monarchy, 'the Crown of Aragon', which was itself a composite monarchy consisting of the kingdoms of Aragon and Valencia and the principality of Catalonia. The population of the Iberian territories of the Crown of Aragon was probably just under one million in the 1520s. The Crown of Aragon also incorporated substantial territories in Italy and the Mediterranean – the great kingdoms of Sicily and Naples and the small islands of the Balearics and Sardinia. It was thus in its own right a Mediterranean and Italian power. Spain's influence in Italy was rounded out in the generation after the Catholic Kings when the Republic of Genoa formed a political and financial alliance with the Spanish crown (1528) and when the duchy of Milan was vested in the crown as an imperial fief (1535). The enormous wealth and military expertise of the Genoese was henceforth exclusively at the service of Charles V, while Milan became the centre from which he mobilized his armies for action throughout Europe.[3]

Nothing, however, so defined the growth of Spanish power as the acquisition of an American empire. In 1492 Castile conquered the Canary Islands and

Mateo Prunes, Map of the Mediterranean, 1563.

The Navigator's Art.

Breue compendio de la sphera y de la arte de nauegar con nueuos instrumentos y reglas, exemplificado con muy subtiles demonstraciones: compuesto por Martin Cortes natural de burjalaroz en el reyno de Aragon y de presente vezino de la ciudad de Cadiz: dirigido al inuictissi mo Monarcha Carlo Quinto Rey de las Hespañas etc. Señor Nuestro.

Ad maximum fortissimum inuictissimumq; Ca rolum Cæsarem huius nominis quintum illephon sus d: sanabria epis dniuasceñ. disticon.

Cæsareo olim iactabas Roma triumphos. Desine dat maius Carolus imperium.

The Navigator's Art.

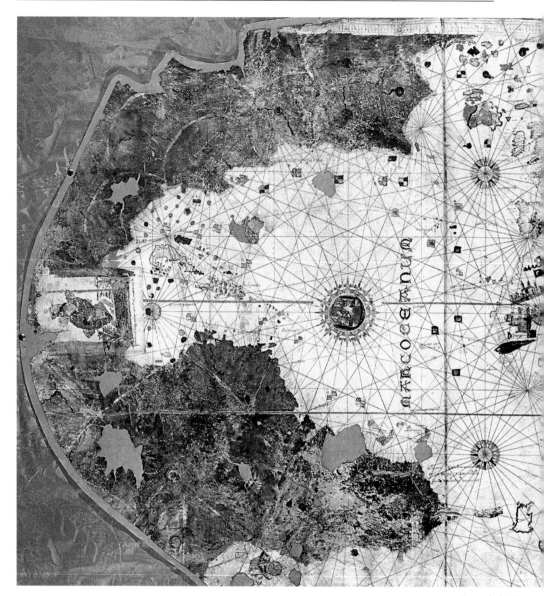

Juan de la Cosa,

acquired a ready-made base for exploration deep into the Atlantic (or the 'Ocean Sea', as Castilians called it). Indeed, Christopher Columbus demonstrated the significance of the Canaries when he used them as a stopping-off point on the momentous voyage of 1492 which brought him to the Americas. The possession of the Canary Islands was fundamental to the ability of Castile to develop and exploit her new possessions, for explorers were able to stop there to repair their ships and to take on fresh victuals – the critical determinant of the length of voyages in the Ocean Sea – and so to shorten the journey across the great sea.

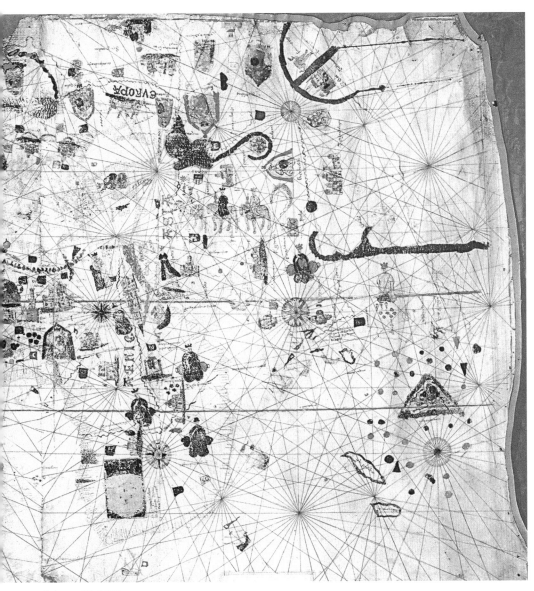

map of the world, 1500.

Columbus made three more voyages to the Americas before he died in 1506, unaware even that he had stumbled across a continent unknown to Europeans. But such was the excitement created by his discoveries that, even by 1500, cartographers were beginning to sketch the 'New World' with accuracy. Among its other consequences, the encounter with America greatly stimulated the study of the sea and of the arts of navigation in Castile.

Columbus's first voyage posed more questions than it solved. The most important among these was that of the rights of the crown of Castile in the

43

Tordesillas.

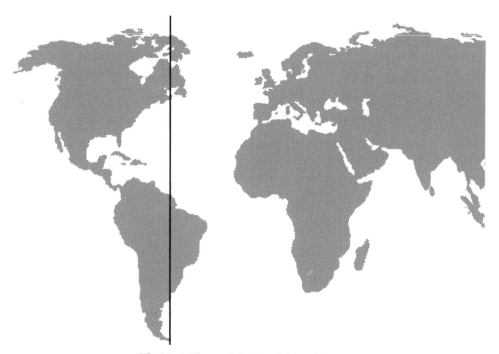

'The Line': The papal division of the world, 1493.

newly-discovered lands. Isabella secured a papal bull (*Inter Caetera*, 1493), which gave the crown of Castile the legal rights in the eyes of the Church to all lands that were more than one hundred leagues (about 1,000 miles) west of an imaginary line drawn from the Azores to the Cape Verde Islands. Sailors of the kingdom of Portugal had rounded Africa exactly as Columbus crossed the Atlantic, and for this reason Portugal was allocated the lands to the east of the papal borderline. In 1494 in the small town of Tordesillas, 21km south of Valladolid, the crowns of Castile and Portugal ratified the papal donation, dividing the Atlantic world between them. To the rest of Europe the division of

Seville: The monopoly port for the Spanish trade with the Americas.

the unknown world seemed to be a matter of little consequence but the Treaty of Tordesillas became one of the landmark treaties of European history, for when it became evident that Columbus had indeed discovered a whole new world it was realized that the papacy – the supreme spiritual authority of the day – had excluded all but Castile and Portugal from it.[4]

In the generation after Columbus's death in 1506, small units of Spanish conquerors (*conquistadores*) overpowered two massive Amerindian empires. Hernan Cortes conquered Aztec Mexico in 1519-21 and renamed it 'New Spain', and Hernando Pizarro and his brothers crushed the Inca kingdom of Peru in the mid-1530s. Both conquests led to wealth beyond even the wildest imaginings of the *conquistadores*. But few of the conquerors were rich for long, for the Castilian government soon overpowered them as they had done the Amerindians. Exactly as the crown did so, in the mid-1540s, the conquest of the Americas entered a dramatic new phase with the discovery of mines producing prodigious amounts of silver. They followed in quick and dramatic succession one after the other: Potosí in Bolivia (1545); Zacatecas in New Spain (1546); Guanajuato, also in New Spain (1558). The crown of Castile was entitled to one fifth (the royal '*quinto*') of all minerals discovered in its territories and so it began to acquire fabulous wealth. But even this was only the beginning. The sixteenth century was a time of great technological advance and the most important improvement in mining was made exactly as the great mines of Spanish America were opened up – the 'mercury-amalgamation process' which allowed the much more rapid separation of silver from ore. The introduction of this process into the mines of New Spain in 1557 marked the beginning of the age of Philip II. From the very outset of his reign, therefore, Philip was to enjoy completely new level of wealth. He was utterly determined to protect and indeed to extend his monopoly. This was true, indeed, even within Spain, for it was Castile that benefited from empire, and the subjects of the Crown of Aragon were normally barred from sailing to the New World just as were Englishmen or

The Tower of Gold, Seville, the reckoning point for cargoes from the New World.

Frenchmen. To protect its colonies, Castile established a monopoly based upon the great southern city of Seville. No one could trade with the Indies, or even sail to or from them, unless they had a passport from the Castilian crown and had registered their ships and cargoes through the Board of Trade and the Consulate (*Casa de la Contratación*, established in 1503; and the *Consulado*, 1543). The cargoes were recorded and unladen at the old Moorish tower named the 'Tower of Gold' on the banks of the River Guadalquivir. As an early priority, Philip developed in the mid-1560s a convoy system designed to bring the treasure home safely each year. Two fleets left Spain for the New World with the goods that the colonists required (and for which they paid in silver). The first, which was known as the *flota*, left for New Spain in the spring and wintered at Vera Cruz. The second, known as the *galeones*, sailed in the autumn and spent the winter at Cartagena. As the fleets sailed from Spain, so the colonial governors were organizing the shipment of silver to the points of collection. The silver from Peru was brought by sea to the Isthmus of Panama and then carried overland on mules to the Caribbean coast; it was then shipped to Havana, where the fleet with the silver from New Spain was waiting for it. The two fleets now joined together to make the homeward journey, accompanied by warships to protect them. They used the Portuguese islands of the Azores as a stopping-off place at which they took on victuals and prepared themselves for the hazardous last leg of the journey. The system was efficient, if cumbersome, and normally the greatest hazards facing the ships were those involved in entering and leaving harbours. But there was a disadvantage: the rhythm of the convoys was known to every sea dog in Europe.[5]

As the Spanish discovered the fabulous silver mines of central and southern America the Portuguese developed their lucrative trades in the luxury goods of Asia – notably in spices, silks and woods – and they developed too the sugar plantations of the coast of Brazil. To work the plantations they imported black slaves from their trading posts on the African coast. The Spanish bought slaves from the Portuguese and in turn developed their own trade. As the two Iberian powers opened up their empires in central and southern America they came to depend increasingly on the labour of enslaved Africans, and as the empires expanded so too did the exploitation until it became what has been called 'the greatest transfer of population and probably the most callous systematic reduction of human beings to commodities in recorded history.'[6] The Portuguese ships were much more vulnerable than the Spanish on their return voyage, for they could not sail in convoys and they were enormously large – often 1,500 tons or more. They too made for the Azores to recover and re-victual before sailing to Lisbon. Carrying prodigiously wealthy cargoes – cumbersome and vulnerable, predictable in their schedules – the Portuguese ships returning from Asia or Brazil were the stuff of dreams for the seamen of northern Europe who were formally excluded from the new worlds.[7]

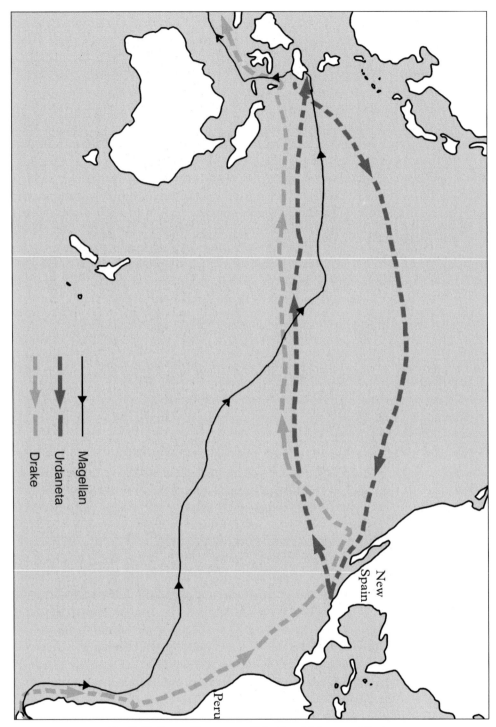

The Pacific Ocean: The voyages of Magellan, Urdaneta and Drake.

Ferdinand Magellan (c.1470-1521).

Magellan's ship: The Victoria.
Magellan sailed from Spain with five ships but only the Victoria reached home safely;
it thus became the first ship to circumnavigate the globe.

The exploitation of the Indies, East and West, still lay very much in the future when the Catholic Kings died, Isabella in 1504 and Ferdinand in 1516. However, the legacy of their brilliant successes passed out of their direct male line and into that of the German house of Habsburg. Their only son, Juan, died in 1496, and so the succession to their kingdoms passed into the female line. The eldest of their four daughters, Juana, was married to Philip of Burgundy, son of the Emperor Maximilian. Juana became queen of Castile on her mother's death but in 1506 her husband died and her fragile mental well-being disintegrated under the strain of her loss. In view of her mental incapacity, her son Charles was proclaimed to be her co-ruler on the throne of Castile even though he was only six years old. When Ferdinand died, he recognized Charles as his successor to the thrones of the Crown of Aragon. Charles thereby became the first person to rule over the whole of Spain, although it is very important to stress that he presided over the constituent parts of the monarchy as sovereign of each of the respective kingdoms. Even this was only the beginning, for in 1519 he was elected to the title of Holy Roman Emperor on the death of his paternal grandfather, the emperor Maximilian I. As emperor, he assumed the title of Charles V, and it was naturally through this title – rather than as Charles I of Spain – that he became known to his contemporaries.

Charles V (1500-58).

Charles came into his various inheritances exactly as the *conquistadores* were laying the basis of Castile's American empire. He therefore enjoyed a unique combination of prestige, power and wealth: as Holy Roman Emperor he exercised nominal authority over much of central and eastern Europe and claimed pre-eminence among the monarchs of Europe while as king of Spain he had the great wealth of the Indies. Indeed, as the great silver mines of the Americas were opened up and exploited in the course of the 1540s, Spain became the most important of Charles's territories, the major financial contributor to the cost of empire.[8]

The accidents of dynastic succession brought Spain into closer contact with the seventeen provinces known as 'the Low Countries' which were also ruled by Charles. There was no formal union between the two territories but the relationship that now developed between them proved to have the most profound and enduring importance. Charles had a special affection for the Low Countries as the land of his birth (1500) but the seventeen provinces that he ultimately came to rule – he acquired three of them as late as the 1540s – were a political unit only in name, for each province had its own laws and traditions, its own political and economic interests. Indeed, they were not even united by a single tongue, for a range of languages and dialects – Dutch, French and German – were spoken. Intensely populated – they had about three million people by the mid-century – they were very rich and had extraordinary strategic and military importance, lying at the very crossroads of northern Europe. Their possession enabled Charles V to exert pressure on France, on the Empire and on England. In an economic sense, the possession of the Low Countries enabled Charles to guard the trade with the Baltic which brought timber and naval supplies to Spain's shipping fleets. Most importantly, he could protect the market to which two-thirds of Castile's wool was sent. He therefore endowed many privileges upon the Low Countries. By the 1550s, Antwerp had developed its status as the greatest trading centre of northern Europe, receiving the goods of central Europe from the Rhine and those of the Baltic, England and Spain by sea. It was also developing as a financial centre of global importance, managing much of the business of the Spanish crown (and therefore receiving great amounts of American silver) and acting as the mart for the luxury goods that the Portuguese brought from Asia and Brazil. England and Spain were further bound together by the vital economic interests that each had in the Low Countries; both exported their wool there to be worked up, both imported the goods of Europe from Antwerp and both depended to a significant extent on the financial services that Antwerp provided. By the time of the accessions of Elizabeth I and Philip II the bonds tying their countries with the prosperity of the Low Countries were of fundamental importance. Both were therefore determined to maintain the prosperity of the Low Countries in order to develop their own economies.[9]

Philip stayed in the Low Countries until the Peace of Cateau-Cambrésis freed him to return to Spain; he sailed for Spain on 25 August 1559. On

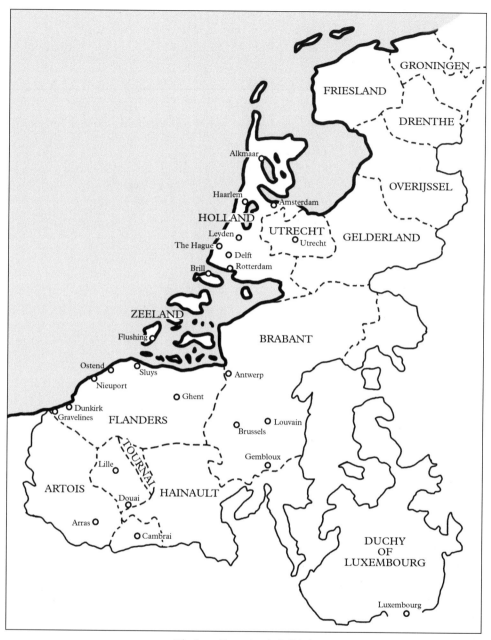

The Low Countries: 1. Political.

arriving home, his first public act was to attend a great *auto de fé* in Valladolid, the city of his birth, in which a number of celebrated heretics were condemned (8 October). Three men were burned alive and nine were garrotted before being fed to the flames as a clemency granted because of their recantation of their sins.[10] As news of the *auto de fé* circulated throughout Europe it seemed only to re-emphasise Philip's commitment to supporting the Inquisition. The reality was more complicated than this, for while Philip undoubtedly did fully support the Inquisition and intended to destroy heresy in Spain he also had as a political priority on his return to bring the Holy Office under royal control. Put simply, it had become too powerful during the long absence of the royal person from the kingdom. Philip needed to demonstrate his support for the Inquisition before he could bring it to heel. But in northern Europe – in England and in the Low Countries in particular – there appeared to be only one common denominator linking the burnings at Smithfield to those at Valladolid. Philip was thus depicted as the very personification of intolerance.[11]

The discovery of cells of an apparently organized Protestant movement in Spain was only the most shocking of the discoveries awaiting Philip on his return in 1559. He also found that the government had pledged all its financial incomes far into the future and had no liquid assets on which it could readily draw for its current expenses. Castile in particular had been drained of resources by the remorseless demands of recent years for taxes with which to pay for Charles V's wars in the north and Philip had therefore to declare a suspension of payments to his bankers in 1560, the second in three years.[12] The ability of the Spanish crown to bankrupt itself even while it enjoyed the unique wealth that came from the Indies puzzled and intrigued many across the face of Europe. Philip himself was bewildered by it and readily confessed that he had no understanding of financial matters – 'I cannot tell a good memorial on the subject from a bad one. And I do not wish to break my brains trying to understand something which I do not understand now nor have ever understood in all my days' – he would write in the 1570s.[13]Philip had also to repair the consequences of Charles V's neglect of Spain; not since 1543 had Spain seen a resident king and the clearest expression of neglect was that the country did not even have a proper capital city; it hardly needed one when the emperor spent so much time abroad. Toledo had served as a capital in recent years but for a variety of reasons it was not appropriate for Philip's needs and in 1561 he chose the small town of Madrid as his new capital. He complemented this by beginning to build in 1563 the great monastery of San Lorenzo del Escorial some 40km to the west of the capital. Together the new capital and the monastery came to provide him with the base from which he re-established the power of the crown. They also served other purposes: in the courtly complex of which Madrid and the Escorial became the centre, Philip became one of the greatest patrons of the arts in European history, most especially in painting and in architecture. But his artistic activities were discreetly managed and news of them did not circulate throughout Europe to balance the impression of the intolerant bigot. Instead, the Escorial became itself part of the Black Legend of Philip II, the forbidding place within whose granite walls Philip plotted to suppress Protestantism and the constitutional freedoms of his subjects.[14]

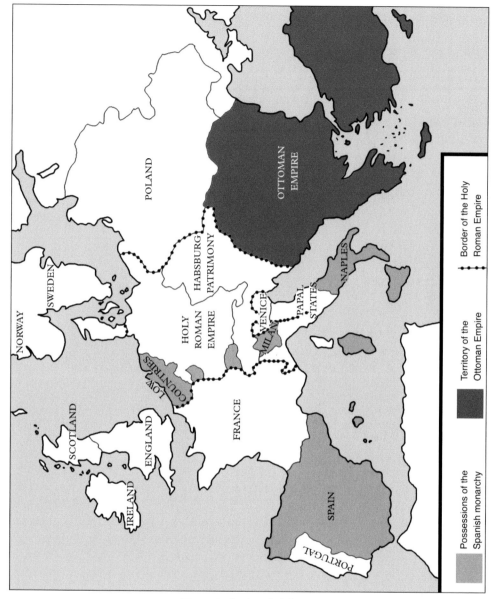

Europe in the Age of Philip II.

The image of Philip as a master of intrigue seemed the more credible because he closely guarded his right to make decisions and he really did find it hard to trust his ministers. Philip had close advisers. He had a deep affection for two of the men who had been his childhood friends – the Portuguese Ruy Gómez de Silva and the Catalan Luis de Requesens. Philip allowed them to exercise important governmental and military roles but the confidence that he had in them was thoroughly exceptional. It most certainly did not extend to the man who had the most powerful personality at court: Don Fernando Álvarez de Toledo, third duke of Alba, had won great victories for both Charles V and Philip and he was not a man to let them forget their debt to him. Alba was an arrogant man, driven by self-confidence which bordered on conviction. But he was also temperamental, given to storming from court when he failed to impose his will. Philip disliked Alba intensely but lacked the self-confidence to do without him and so he repeatedly summoned him back to court. He could neither control Alba nor do without him. It was demeaning to his kingship.[15]

In the early years after his return to Spain, Philip's chief preoccupation lay in the Mediterranean rather in northern Europe. He inherited a situation in which Spanish power in the Mediterranean was wilting in the face of an onslaught by Ottoman Turkey (under its great leader, Suleiman the Magnificent) and its allies operating out of the pirate bases of Tripoli and Algiers. A series of disasters reduced Philip's galley fleet from ninety-one ships in 1559 to fifty-two in 1564. He undertook a great galley-building programme and coerced his allies into helping him. Most especially, he persuaded successive popes to allow him to tax the Castilian church to help fund his new fleet. By 1574 he was supporting 147 galleys and had been able to stem the tide of Islamic advance, most notably when in 1565 he managed to relieve Malta from a brutal siege by the Turks and in 1571 when he led an alliance of the papacy and the Republic of Venice to a devastating victory over the full might of the Turkish fleet at the battle of Lepanto. In doing so he demonstrated that he could both build a great fleet and deploy it effectively.[16] He also established himself as the leader of Christian Europe. Even Elizabeth of England congratulated him.[17]

3 Breakdown: The Queen of Scots, the Privateer and the Iron Duke

By the middle of the 1560s three issues were beginning to strain relations between England and Spain: the uncertainties surrounding the succession to the English throne; the resentments aroused by Philip's determination to exclude English seamen from his territories in the Americas; and the disquiet felt in London about his resolve to crush the rebellion in the Low Countries. These issues each found their embodiments in extraordinary personalities – the questions over the succession revolved upon the challenge to Elizabeth by Mary Stuart, the Catholic and pro-French queen of Scots; the English incursion into the American seas was spearheaded by Francis Drake, a privateer of brilliance who at times seemed to be fighting a private war with the king of Spain; and the Spanish determination to crush rebellion in the Low Countries was in the hands of the fearsome duke of Alba. Relations between London and Madrid were further embittered by Elizabeth's treatment of the Catholic minority in England and by Philip's relentless persecution of Protestantism in the Low Countries. The potent mixture of politics, religion and trading rights had by the end of the 1570s brought England and Spain to the brink of war. However, up until 1580, appearance had been in many respects more important than reality. Elizabeth and Philip were engaged in a struggle for prestige in which the threat of force was more important than the actual use of it. The occasional demonstration of military excellence, whether on land or at sea, would prevent the outbreak of full-scale hostility; it would also be much cheaper. Both monarchs deployed their best commanders and forces in an effort to make the other see the terrible consequences of a final rupture; Elizabeth's privateers achieved remarkable feats, but the greatest among them only sailed at intervals of three or four or even five years; Philip threatened to use his awesome Army of Flanders to invade England but made only tentative preparations to do so.

While Philip was concentrating on his struggle with the Turk in the Mediterranean, Elizabeth was confronting the difficulties created by her own unmarried state and the threat posed by Mary Stuart. In 1560 she sent an army and a fleet to help expel the French from Scotland; the operation was brilliantly successful and by the Treaty of Edinburgh in July the French agreed to withdraw from Scotland. However, in that same year Mary Stuart was widowed by the death of Francis II and in 1561 returned to Scotland at the invitation of nobles who wanted her support against the growing power of the

Pedro Menéndez de Avilés (1519-74)

Presbyterians. In the harsh world of Scottish politics, Mary's sex was as much a handicap as her Catholic religion. She married twice, the first time badly (Henry, Lord Darnley: 1565), the second disastrously (James Hepburn, earl of Bothwell: 1567). Both husbands were violent men. In 1566 Darnley had Mary's secretary, David Rizzio, murdered because he suspected him of having an affair with the queen. Mary took cold revenge; she waited until she had given birth in June 1566 to Darnley's son – the future James VI of Scotland and James I of England – and then had him assassinated. The deed was almost certainly organized by Bothwell, and when Mary promptly married him she was driven from the throne for a second time. To save her life, she fled to England in May 1568.

The presence of Mary Stuart in England changed English politics structurally. Exactly as it became evident that Elizabeth (who was now thirty-five years of age) would not produce an heir, the woman who had the strongest legal claim to succeed her arrived in England. Although Mary was placed under house arrest – for her own protection, according to Elizabeth – she continued to insist on her right to the succession and began to cultivate her position as figurehead for the growing number of Catholics who were anxious about their future in England. For nearly two decades, Mary Stuart laid claim to the loyalty of Catholic Englishmen and to the support of Catholic Europe in her attempts to overthrow Elizabeth. Her numerous intrigues – for Mary was the most compulsive of plotters – would invariably culminate in Elizabeth's death, but ultimately they made her own execution inevitable.[1]

The first sailors to test the solidity of the Castilian monopoly in the Caribbean were French Huguenots. In 1555 Jacques de Sores occupied Havana for a month and in 1562 and 1564 the Huguenot leader, Admiral Coligny, dispatched expeditions which founded small settlements in Florida. Philip dealt swiftly and brutally with the threat; in September 1565, his trusted admiral, Pedro Menéndez de Avilés, slaughtered the French settlers and then founded Fort St Agustin, the first Spanish settlement on North American soil. Philip was especially gratified by the success and had his ambassador in England inform Queen Elizabeth of what had happened.[2]

Philip's tacit warning to Elizabeth was well-judged, for the English were beginning to intrude in significant numbers into the Castilian monopoly. The first Englishman to capture a Spanish treasure ship seems to have been Robert Reneger of Southampton in 1545 and within ten years a significant number of seamen were taking the risks involved in hunting for Spanish vessels. In 1556 two large English ships were captured off the south-west coast of Spain as they lay in waiting for stray treasure ships, and in 1561 no fewer than five English corsair ships were taken off Madeira. Two factors encouraged English seamen to become more adventurous in their pursuit of Spanish treasure: the papal division of the world was no longer relevant to them because of their own rejection of Roman Catholic authority, while the failure of the peacemakers at

Cateau-Cambrésis to legislate for events in the Americas – 'beyond the line' – meant that there was no legal reason why the English should not press ahead with their ventures in the New World.

The first major confrontation between the Spanish and the English in the Caribbean came in 1568. John Hawkins of Plymouth made lucrative voyages to the Caribbean to sell black African slaves to the colonists (1562-3 and 1564-5) but when in 1567 he began planning another voyage his preparations were monitored by the Spanish embassy in London. Soon Philip knew every detail of the expedition – that Hawkins was sailing with nine ships, and eight hundred chosen men. Most importantly of all, Philip knew that four of the ships belonged to the Queen herself, including the flagship, the *Jesus of Lubeck*. That Elizabeth was investing so heavily – and so openly – in the expedition gave the lie to her protestations of friendship to Spain and made it imperative that Philip take the very firmest action to deal with the threat posed by Hawkins. He put his agents in the Caribbean on alert and ordered them to deal sternly with the interloper.[3]

When Hawkins sailed into the Caribbean with 400 African slaves he found that the settlers were too intimidated to trade with him and that he had to force them to do so at the point of a gun. As he sailed home his little fleet was twice hit by storms off Cuba and he ran before the wind to the port of San Juan de Ulúa, to take refuge so that he could repair his ships. As he approached the port, on 15 September 1568, he found to his astonishment that he was welcomed by the port authorities, who believed that his ships were the fleet bringing the new viceroy of New Spain, Don Martín Enríquez de Almansa. Hawkins accepted safe harbour before the authorities were able to rectify their mistake, and when Enríquez de Almansa's fleet duly appeared, Hawkins refused to let it enter the port unless the viceroy guaranteed the safe conduct of the English fleet. Terms were agreed, and the Spanish fleet berthed in the harbour on 21 September. Hawkins and Enríquez both knew that the issue between them would be resolved by battle, and on 23 September a short but vicious fight began. The English sank the viceroy's *capitana* and burned his *almiranta* but lost three of their own ships – the *Angel* and the *Swallow* went to the bottom and the *Jesus of Lubeck* was damaged beyond repair. While Hawkins was leading the fight to save his fleet, his young kinsman Francis Drake escaped from the harbour with his own ship: he 'forsooke us in our myserie', as Hawkins unforgivingly put it. Hawkins managed to fight his way out of the harbour but the shortage of provisions forced him to abandon 114 of his men to find their fate in New Spain and he himself finally made it home to England, arriving in February 1569.[4] He found that Drake had already reached Plymouth, and although intense bitterness now divided the two men, they joined together in declamations of anger about the treachery of the Spanish at San Juan de Ulúa. Of course they both had their own reasons for doing so – Drake to excuse his flight; Hawkins to justify the failure of an expedition of which Queen was a major sponsor. But beneath the rhetoric both men realized

Margaret of Parma (1522-86).

that the ships in which they had sailed had been unequal to the tasks they demanded of them and began to think seriously about the improvements that needed to be made to the ships if they were to sail again into the Caribbean, as indeed they were determined to do. From these deliberations a new form of vessel was born: one that fully exploited its artillery and was swift and highly manoeuvrable.

The third major cause of the breakdown in Anglo-Spanish friendship lay in the revolt that broke out in the Low Countries in the mid-1560s against Philip's rule. When Philip sailed away from the Low Countries in 1559 he left his half-sister Margaret of Parma as Regent, with Bishop Granvelle as her first minister. He gave them a clearly considered programme: they were not to involve the local aristocracy in government; they were to restructure the Church to make it more efficient by increasing the number of bishoprics; they were to crush religious dissidence and to act in major affairs only on instructions from Madrid. A nine-year grant – the 'Novennial Aid' – was won from the Estates and so Margaret and Granvelle had a breathing-space until it expired in 1567 in which they could achieve the last of Philip's orders – to make the Low Countries financially independent of Spain. Philip undoubtedly meant to return to the Low Countries but he never did so; year after year he

Antoine Perrenot, Cardinal Granvelle (1517-86).

was detained by the needs of Spain. The stern policies that he had bequeathed to Margaret and Granvelle might have been designed to inflame resentments across the face of Netherlands society for they threatened many vested interests – aristocratic and plebeian; Catholic and Protestant. The government's first defeat came as early as 1561 when Philip was forced to agree to the removal of the Spanish troops that were the mainstay of the royal government. Worse followed; concerted action by aristocratic leaders – notably the counts of

Violencias y Sacrilegios que los C de Amberez

The Iconoclastic Riots in Antwerp, 20 August 1566.

Egmont and Hornes and the prince of Orange – led to the dismissal of Granvelle in March 1564.

The removal of his chief minister was the point of no return for Philip. He decided that he would not retreat further, and on 17 and 20 October 1565 wrote two seminal letters to Margaret which he signed in 'the Woods of Segovia'. These letters insisted that no compromise was to be allowed on religious matters and that no restraints were to be placed upon the Inquisition. Moreover, no meaningful consultation was to take place with the great nobles. Opposition now was led by the lesser nobles; at the end of the year some four hundred of them joined together to write 'The Compromise of the Nobility', and on 5 April 1566 two hundred of them forced themselves into the presence of Margaret and thrust their 'Request' upon her. It spoke of 'an open revolt and a universal rebellion' against the rule of the king. Margaret crumbled under pressure; she suspended the operation of the decrees against heresy and announced that she would ask Philip to adopt a less stern policy.[5]

Margaret's weakness encouraged all the opponents of the crown but when rebellion broke out in the summer of 1566 it was not aristocratic and political but popular and religious. Hundreds of 'hedge-preachers' roamed the country instigating riots which struck at everything that the Roman Catholic Church held dear; thousands of statues and images were destroyed or damaged and hundreds of churches, convents and monasteries were attacked. On 31 July 1566 Philip once again fired off a batch of letters from his retreat in the woods of Segovia, but this time he gave way before the storm. He agreed to abolish the Inquisition in the Low Countries and to offer a general pardon to those who had rebelled against him. He promised that he would come to the provinces to settle affairs: 'I will not fail to come, please God. I expect to be with you at the latest next spring, and if there is a way of going earlier, be sure that I won't fail to use it'.[6]

Philip was in fact trying to buy time, for he was determined now to strike back at his rebellious subjects. He decided, with the support of his councillors of State, to raise a substantial army and to send it to the Low Countries and to follow this up by visiting the provinces himself. Ostensibly, therefore, the army would prepare the way for his own arrival as a benign prince who was prepared to forgive his rebellious subjects. In reality, of course, Philip's intention was only to go the Low Countries himself after the army had reasserted control and meted out punishment to rebels and malefactors. Any doubt about the real purpose of the army disappeared when Alba himself accepted command of it in November 1566. It took the 'Iron Duke' some months to prepare the army, but on 22 August 1567 he entered Brussels at the head of 10,000 men, the elite corps of what was to become the 'Army of Flanders'. Alba immediately established a tribunal to punish wrongdoers and to cow the people of the Low Countries; it at once started work, handing down death sentences by the score. Not even the highest in the land were safe from Alba; as a dreadful warning to all, the counts of Egmont and Hornes were beheaded in Brussels square on

Fernando Álvarez de Toledo, 3rd duke of Alba, (1509-82).

charges of treason (5 June 1568). Both men had held the highest positions in the land and had served Philip with distinction; the lesson of their deaths was clear for all to see.[7]

The brutality of Alba's regime did not cause Elizabeth to budge from her stated position that the rebellion in the Low Countries was unlawful and could not be supported, for she was genuinely horrified by the sight of a gathering revolt against a lawful monarch. She was also more afraid of a pro-French Netherlands than she was of a Spanish-controlled one. But if Elizabeth would not support rebellion against Philip in the Low Countries she was quite prepared to take indirect action in order to increase his difficulties. The opportunity to do so presented itself when in December 1568 some Spanish galleons carrying treasure for the payment of the Army of Flanders took refuge in English ports from the twin threats of storms and Huguenot ships. Elizabeth took the treasure into her own safekeeping while she established – as she claimed – to whom it really belonged. She spoke 'sweet words' to the Spanish ambassador and promised to restore the treasure but quite failed to do so, aware that every day's delay heightened Alba's difficulties in paying his troops.[8] Alba reciprocated by imposing an embargo on English trade with the Low Countries and Elizabeth promptly banned Philip's ships from trading in her ports. At the height of the dispute, Hawkins and Drake returned with their emotive tales of Spanish treachery at San Juan de Ulua.

Philip was outraged by Elizabeth's seizure of his treasure and in February 1569 he wrote to Alba of 'the good opportunity which now presents itself to remedy religious affairs in that country by deposing the present Queen and giving the crown to the queen of Scotland'. He gave Alba permission to 'take the steps that you consider advisable'. In effect, Phlip was inviting Alba to invade England to overthrow Elizabeth. The duke refused to do so and at the end of 1569 Philip wrote again: 'we are beginning to lose reputation by deferring so long to provide a remedy for the great grievance done by this woman to my subjects, friends, and allies'.[9] The pope also pressed Alba to act to relieve the position of the English Catholics and to place Mary Stuart on the throne (3 November 1569). Still, Alba refused to act. He pointed out that Philip would need to raise three fleets if he seriously intended to invade England – one to actually mount the invasion and two to defend the Straits and the coasts of Spain against the French.[10] In February 1570 Alba wrote to Philip urging him to remember that wars were always more easily started than they were finished, and insisting that if an invasion of England was to be mounted it would cost a very great deal of money. He added that 'money is the nerve of war' and suggested that if Philip seriously wanted him to invade England he should give him the enormous resources that would be required to do so.[11] The most senior general in Europe had declared that the invasion of England was not really a viable possibility. There the matter rested, at least for the moment.

One other possibility began to present itself exactly as Philip lost patience with Elizabeth. In 1569, Bishop Maurice of Cassel arrived in Madrid to negotiate on behalf of Irish Catholic nobles for military support against England. Philip was much taken by the prospect and mused in a letter to Alba that if it did come to war with England, God was offering Ireland as a base to Spain.[12] The tantalizing prospect of repaying Elizabeth in Ireland for the support she was giving to his rebels in the Low Countries tempted Philip for the remainder of his reign.

As Philip and Alba tried to persuade each other to take action against Elizabeth, a revolt against her actually broke out in the north of England. The dukes of Westmoreland and Northumberland feared that Elizabeth was destroying their seigneurial power as she extended that of the crown and they also became involved in an intrigue to marry Mary Stuart to the duke of Norfolk, England's premier earl. The government knew most of what was being plotted and when the two earls were summoned to London to explain themselves, they rode instead to Durham cathedral and raised the banner of rebellion by celebrating mass (14 November 1569).[13] Elizabeth's response was efficient and it was brutal: Mary Stuart was moved to a place of safety beyond reach of the rebels and the rebellion was quickly put down. Some 700 people were executed, among them Northumberland himself. Westmoreland escaped to the Low Countries. The north would not revolt again and Spain's best chance of fomenting (or taking advantage of) a Catholic rebellion in England had gone.

Pius V grandly ignored the failure of the rebellion to confer what he took to be his support on the English Catholics. On 20 February 1570 he issued the bull *Regnans in Excelsis*, by which he deposed Elizabeth and made it legitimate for Catholics to disobey her and even to plot her overthrow and death. Philip was furious with the pope. He wrote to Elizabeth, exculpating himself of responsibility for Pius's action and informed his ambassador in England of his fears that this 'sudden and unexpected step will exacerbate feeling there, and drive the Queen and her friends the more to oppress and persecute the few good Catholics still remaining in England'.[14] Philip's judgement was correct. The papal bull, issued after a rebellion that had failed totally, forced English Catholics to balance their loyalty to their Queen against their commitment to their faith and it made every English Catholic vulnerable to the charge of treason, real or potential.

Moreover, the failure of the Northern Rebellion forced Mary Stuart herself to look increasingly to the assassination of Elizabeth for her own salvation; from 1570, Mary was involved in one such plot after another. The first of them involved Roberto Ridolfi, a Florentine banker who was known to the English government as an inveterate and not very competent plotter. A letter was found in his possession from the papal nuncio in Paris promising that papal funds would be made available to support a Spanish invasion of England. The plan was not much more than a broad sketch but the queen of Scots was beguiled

Sir Francis Walsingham (1532-90).

by it. Unfortunately, the English spymaster, Francis Walsingham, knew everything that was afoot, and indeed may even have been playing the role of *agent provocateur* to entrap Mary. Walsingham was able to prove that the Earl of Norfolk and the Spanish ambassador, Guerau de Espés, were both involved in the plot. Norfolk was arrested in September 1571 and after much agonizing on Elizabeth's part, he was beheaded on 2 June 1572. Elizabeth refused to execute a fellow-monarch, and so Mary Stuart survived. With each new plot, however, the pressure from Parliament increased on the queen – to marry; to persecute Roman Catholics vigorously; to execute Mary Stuart. The English Catholics became especially vulnerable: Parliament passed the Treasons Act in 1571 which made it high treason to deny the Royal Supremacy or to call the queen a heretic.[15]

In the spring of 1572 Elizabeth closed English ports to a small band of Dutch rebel seamen who had been preying on Spanish shipping in the Channel; their activities had also disturbed the trade of English merchants and thus provoked Elizabeth to move against them. At all events, on 1 April 1572 a small flotilla of these ships landed at the Brill in Zeeland; finding it undefended, they established a base there. A week later they repeated the exercise at Flushing; this was a major acquisition, for it was the only deep-water port on the Dutch coast. The acquisition of these two sea-towns provided the rebels in the Low Countries with ports out of which they could operate and through which they could readily receive reinforcements and supplies. The revolt spread like wildfire in the north; by the autumn, only Middelburg and Amsterdam remained in Spanish hands. Alba's lack of a naval force rebounded upon him; his great army could do little against the ships of the 'Sea Beggars' (as the rebels became known) and the inadequacy of the Spanish navy in the Low Countries revealed itself in a succession of defeats inflicted by rebel squadrons – in November 1572 off Flushing itself; in October 1573 in the Zuider Zee and in January 1574 in the eastern Scheldt. Worse followed: in February 1574 Middelburg capitulated after a two-year siege and in May the last Spanish inshore squadron was defeated. The rebels now controlled the inland waterways of Holland and Zeeland.[16] The nature of the revolt had changed, dramatically and enduringly, with the acquisition of effective sea power by the rebels.

But even with their new maritime strength, the rebels needed support from abroad, and since Elizabeth refused to give such sustenance they had to hope for French aid. The prospect of this disintegrated when on 23–24 August 1572 – the night of St Bartholomew's Day – Catherine de' Medici organized the assassination of Admiral Coligny and the slaughter of 2,000 of his Huguenot supporters in Paris where they were assembled for the wedding of Henry of Navarre. Imitative massacres took place at once in many regional cities and it seemed as if the Huguenot party in France was in danger of being crushed.

Philip had not organized the Massacre of St Bartholomew's Day but he certainly benefited from it, for he no longer had to fear that France would come to the aid of the rebels in the Low Countries. Freed of the need to watch his back for a French invasion, Alba now set out on a systematic campaign of terror, besieging carefully-selected towns and slaughtering their garrisons when they surrendered.[17] But Alba's brutality was counterproductive, for it only made his opponents the more determined not to yield to him. It therefore made the war into one of brutal and lengthy sieges. This in turn was enormously expensive. Alba had tried to raise taxes locally with a variety of property taxes but he had failed and the costs of his campaign were largely borne by the Castilian taxpayers; of the 4,362,916 ducats that the government received in 1572-3, no less than 3,455,119 (79%) came from Castile.[18] Philip had sent Alba to the Low Countries to bring rebellion to an end and to make the provinces self-sufficient financially; the duke had failed in both respects – and on a colossal scale.

Philip named the Duke of Medinaceli to replace Alba but he proved inadequate for the task and so Philip appointed Don Luis de Requesens in his stead. Don Luis took the post only very reluctantly; he was named on 30 January 1573 but not until 17 November did he arrive in Brussels.[19] His appointment represented a radical shift of policy by the king, for Philip now accepted that the war in the Low Countries had to be brought to a conclusion, if need be by winning a favourable position from which he could negotiate with the rebels. To do so, Philip gave Requesens more resources than even Alba had commanded: by March 1574 the Army of Flanders numbered 86,235 men and its budget for 1574 of 3,977,151 ducats was twice as large as that of the preceding year.[20] But even this was not enough, for the men of the Army of Flanders had not been paid for several years and demanded the immediate settlement of this backlog. On 15 April 1574 Requesens's veteran Spanish soldiers mutinied and he had to pay them some of their arrears to prevent them from sacking Antwerp. There seemed no way in which Philip could extricate himself from the quagmire of the Low Countries; even as he greatly increased the resources available to Requesens, the situation continued to spiral out of control.

As Philip reflected on the worsening situation in the Low Countries he received a paper from a Dr Sandero postulating that the Queen of England was fighting – and winning – a war with him without herself taking any of the risks or costs of battle. Sandero insisted that it was Elizabeth's support for the rebels that was making them more determined to fight on against Spain – a condition of the war by proxy and privateer in which the two monarchs were engaged.[21] Sandero's paper contained some painful truths and may well have helped to confirm Philip in his determination to send a substantial fleet to protect Spanish shipping in the Channel and to capture some ports in the Low Countries so that Spanish infantry could be ferried there. Philip appointed the redoubtable Pedro Menéndez de Avilés as Captain General of the fleet on 10 February 1574.[22] The purpose of the fleet was not made known, and in all probability Philip was still reflecting on its deployment as he assembled it. Certainly, he intended that Menéndez de Avilés should transport a sizeable infantry force to the Low Countries. The fleet might well serve other purposes, and Elizabeth herself certainly feared that Philip intended to use it to attack

Luis Requesens (1528-76).

England; she armed twenty-eight of her own ships and forty private vessels under the command of Lord Howard of Effingham.

Elizabeth would certainly have been deeply alarmed had she known of another paper to arrive on Philip's desk in 1574, for in June he received a report from Diego Ortíz de Urízar, whom he had sent to Ireland to investigate whether Menéndez de Avilés might find a base there from which he could operate in the Channel. In June, Ortíz de Urízar reported back to Philip with a plan to invade Ireland; it would, he informed Philip, be an easy operation to mount and he advised him that 'whoever wants to take England should begin in Ireland'.[23]

Whatever plans Philip was formulating for his fleet, they came to nothing. When Menéndez de Avilés took command of the fleet on 8 September 1574 it was certainly a formidable force, consisting of 150 sail and 12,000 men. But on the very same day, Menéndez collapsed with fever. He died a week later and Philip abandoned the idea of sending the fleet into the Channel. In the following year he tried once again to send troops to the Low Countries by sea in a small fleet under Pedro de Valdés. However, the fleet sailed late in September and ran into a storm off Ushant. Some of Valdés's ships were even forced to take refuge in English ports.[24]

The two fleets of 1574 and 1575 indicated the way in which Philip's mind was beginning to turn; clearly he intended to establish a naval presence in the Channel to protect some of the vital interests of his monarchy, and clearly, too, he intended to deal with the threat to his shipping posed by English and French shipping. Unable to find a way forward in the Low Countries and unwilling to retreat from his commitment to the military subjugation of the rebels, Philip sent nearly 5,000,000 ducats to the Low Countries in 1575. In doing so he devastated his own finances; on 1 September he declared a suspension of payments to his bankers for the third time in the reign. A few months later, on 5 March 1576, he lost his Governor General when Requesens died. There seemed no solution to the problems created for him by the revolt in the Low Countries.

As Philip began to ponder on the need to build up his naval forces, Elizabeth was already carrying out a major shipbuilding programme. From the very beginning of her reign Elizabeth showed an intuitive understanding of the need to defend herself and her realm through the use of naval power. In the year of her accession Elizabeth established a commission of enquiry to investigate the condition of the navy. The commission advised her that England needed a fleet of twenty-four ships ranging between 200-800 tons, four barks of 60-80 tons and two pinnaces of 40 tons; a total of thirty ships. Elizabeth asked her first parliament for money for 'the continual maintenance of the English Navy' so that it could 'be ever in readiness against all evil happs; the strongest wall and defence that can be against the enemies of this island'. The enemies that Elizabeth had chiefly in mind were the French. So that the navy could be properly organized and controlled, Elizabeth developed the structure of the Navy Board, ordering it to meet at least once a week and to report to the Lord Admiral. She developed the principle that a dozen or so ships should be always on standby to be ready for mobilization at a fortnight's notice and had the officers of the Navy Board work towards standardizing guns on her ships and organizing a system for providing victuals in time of war and peace. In providing for the navy,

Queen Elizabeth (1533-1603), Federico Zuccaro.
This lyrical study of the Queen is perhaps the freest of all portraits of her. Zuccaro had the unique distinction of
working for both Elizabeth and Philip II (for whom he worked in the Escorial).

Sir John Hawkins (1532-95), Hieronymous Custodis.

Oquendo's Standard.

Elizabeth broke with her habitual parsimony: in the years 1564-74 she spent about 6.5% of her income on the navy.[25]

Her greatest efforts were concentrated on the ships themselves; it was no coincidence that the invasion scares of 1574 and 1575 were followed by what proved to be the key decade in the development of the gun-carrying warship. From the time of the incident at San Juan de Ulúa, John Hawkins had been convinced that England needed to build a new sort of warship that would serve a number of different purposes – to sail long distances but to fight at close quarters; to manoeuvre quickly and alter direction suddenly so that all of its many guns could be brought to bear in unceasing cadence upon the enemy; to be able to stand firm in the water while the guns were fired; to have strong decks to support its heavy guns and the pressures created by their recoil. These technologies came together in the new warship of the middle of the sixteenth century. The English led the way in the development of what is normally described as 'the galleon', the gun-carrying man-of-war. It has been observed that the term should properly apply to a ship which 'combined the forepart of a galley with the afterpart of a ship'.[26] The galleon had a longer hull in proportion to the beam than was normal. It mounted two heavy chase guns under the low forecastle, and for battle itself the English favoured the culverin, which had a long range but carried a comparatively light shot. But they had their share of heavy bronze guns which could cause serious damage to enemy ships. The galleon was a manoeuvrable ship that fired modern guns ahead and carried a heavy complement of guns on its broadside. The ship was built longer and slimmer to sail more quickly and the reduction in the two castles made for a longer gun deck.

Some old ships were rebuilt to the new design, among them the *Bull* and the *Tiger* but the first ship to be purpose-built as a fighting galleon was completed in 1573 and was named the *Dreadnought*. It displaced some 700 tons but carried 31 tons of ordnance, 4.5% of the weight of the ship. This was an unprecedented proportion of gun-to-ship. The *Dreadnought* was the first of many such ships; in 1573 it was followed by the *Achates* and the *Handmaid*; in 1577 by the *Revenge* and *Scout*; in 1580-81 by the *Swallow*, the *Elizabeth Bonaventure*, *Antelope* and *Lion* (which was re-built); and in 1584 by the *Nonpareil*. By the later 1570s, therefore, the English state was producing a new sort of ship for its defence, and in 1586, exactly as Philip II began to prepare his great fleet in Lisbon, Elizabeth built three more ships. In 1587 she bought the newly-built *Ark Royal* from Sir Walter Raleigh. She thus had the basis of her war-fleet for 1588.[27]

Elizabeth and her ministers took care, too, to train the men who would work both rigs and guns in close combat. These were often highly technical operations and all sailors had to be able to turn their hand to all of them. The new ships therefore were manned by highly accomplished seamen – and there were many of them, for the Elizabethan navy had begun to sacrifice the number of soldiers so that it could carry more sailors. By 1585 perhaps 10% of the men serving on the new warships were gunners.[28]

Philip replaced Requesens with his own half-brother, Don John of Austria. Don John's reputation as a warrior was unrivalled but Philip could no longer afford to make war and sent the great soldier in the hope that his reputation alone would encourage the enemy to sue for peace. By the time Don John arrived in the Low Countries his own army was out of control. At the end of July the mutinous troops started to pillage loyalist towns, and in doing so alienated many of the crown's staunchest supporters. On 3 November, about 3,500 troops of the Army of Flanders began to systematically plunder the great city of Antwerp. In eleven days some 7,500 people died and many important buildings were destroyed, including even some Catholic churches and religious foundations.[29]

The 'Spanish Fury' at Antwerp shattered the legitimacy of Spanish rule in the Low Countries, and even while the sack of the city was in progress, the States-General of the loyalist provinces signed the 'Pacification of Ghent' with the rebel provinces of Holland and Zeeland, insisting that Spanish troops be withdrawn and that the ancient privileges be guaranteed. William of Orange was named as Stadholder of Holland and Zeeland. The operation of the Placards was suspended and the religious status quo was recognized. This meant in practice that Calvinism was recognized as the legitimate religion of Holland and Zeeland. Don John had no room for manoeuvre and on 12 February 1577 he issued the 'Perpetual Edict' agreeing that Spanish troops would leave within a few weeks and accepting the terms of the Pacification of Ghent. In April 1577 the Spanish troops marched out of the Low Countries. On 6 May Don John took the oath as Governor-General of the Low Countries.

In all probability Don John was not particularly interested in the Low Countries. He was dreaming of winning a kingdom for himself by freeing Mary Stuart and making her queen of England, himself becoming king. Elizabeth was well aware of the Governor-General's romantic plotting, and made sure that it brought very real consequences for one figure: the Spanish ambassador to England was imprisoned in the Tower of London, accused of acting as a link between Don John, Mary Queen of Scots and the English Catholics. Elizabeth sent Thomas Wilkes to Madrid to urge that Don John be replaced and that the Pacification be used as the basis of a settlement.[30]

But Philip was in no position to make a settlement, for he was betrayed by a member of his own family when his nephew, the Archduke Matthias, accepted the sovereignty of the Low Countries from the States General. Philip was forced to go back to war in order to counter his nephew's treachery. He sent 3,000 Spanish troops back to the Low Countries under his nephew Alexander Farnese, the son of Margaret of Parma. It is not clear that Philip had any great opinion of Farnese's military capacities, but it was imperative that he have a member of his own family lead the troops in order to give the lie to Matthias's presumption. On 31 January 1578 Farnese defeated the forces of the States at Gembloux. Undecided whether he could fight a major campaign in the Low Countries, Philip instructed his new ambassador in England, Don Bernardino de Mendoza, to do all that he could to prevent Elizabeth from giving aid to the rebels – he instructed him to 'continue to deal gently and amiably with the Queen'. It did not come easily to Mendoza, for he was a belligerent and aggressive man, a soldier who had little time for the arts of diplomacy.[31]

Elizabeth's response to the deterioration in relations with Spain was to send Francis Drake off on what became a voyage of circumnavigation of the globe. Drake left Plymouth on 13 December 1577 with four ships and 164 men. It seems likely that the journey had its origin in a plan by Richard Greville to found a colony in South America. Certainly, Drake was sponsored by the Queen herself and by the leading members of the war-party at court, notably Walsingham and Leicester. He headed across the Atlantic but not to the Caribbean; he sailed down the coast of South America and at the end of August 1578 entered Magellan's Straits. After a fortnight he entered the Pacific and was greeted by a monstrous storm which flung his little ship around for a month.

As Francis Drake entered the Pacific Ocean and Alexander Farnese began his career in the Low Countries, the king of Portugal embarked on a crusade against the infidel. King Sebastian, the son of Philip's sister Juana, led his army to destruction at Alcazarquivir in Morocco on 3 August 1578; only 100 men of a force of 17,000 escaped to return home. The throne passed to Cardinal Henry,

Alexander Farnese (1545-92).

Francis Drake (1543-96), Marcus Gheeraerts the Younger.
This fine portrait shows the brilliant pirate as the gentleman that he so wanted to be.

an aged epileptic, who had no heirs and was very unlikely to live long. Philip had the best claim to the throne, through his mother. His chief rivals were Catarina, Duchess of Braganza, and Antonio, Prior of Crato – the one was handicapped by her sex, the other by his illegitimacy. Philip dispatched two of his most trusted ministers to press his claim to the throne – Pedro Téllez Giron, first duke of Osuna, and Christovão de Moura, Secretary of the Council of State.

The Golden Hinde.

The first English ship to circumnavigate the globe, the Golden Hinde *was a mere 60ft long in the hull and 75ft at the waterline.*

Don John died from typhus on 1 October 1578. He was only thirty-three years of age. On his deathbed he named Alexander Farnese to succeed him. Farnese had proved himself to be a general of substance when in June he captured Maastricht and he now demonstrated his mastery of the political arts, persuading the states of Artois, Hainault and Douai to form the Union of Arras (6 January 1579) and to return to their loyalty to Philip on his assurance that no Spanish troops would be billeted upon them. The north replied in kind. On 29 January 1579 the Union of Utrecht was signed between the states of Holland and Zeeland and Friesland, Utrecht, Gelderland and the Ommelanden of Groningen. They undertook to continue the war. This was a Protestant, rebellious league. On 15 June 1580 Philip put a price on the head of William of Orange.

As he did so, Francis Drake took the war into the Pacific. He sacked Valparaiso (5 December 1578) and in March captured the *Nuestra Senora de la*

Buckland Abbey.
Drake bought the Abbey at Buckland with the proceeds from his capture of the Cacafuego *off the South American coast. The pirate had turned landowner, and in the year after his return from the circumnavigation he became Lord Mayor of Plymouth. For five years (1580-85) he did not sail again.*

Concepción, known as the *Cacafuego*, a royal treasure ship. After sailing to California, Drake then headed west across the Pacific. He completed the first circumnavigation since the voyage of Magellan and Del Cano fifty years before. The queen's share of the booty was £300,000 – equivalent to more than a year's ordinary income. She used the windfall to pay off her entire foreign debt and still had some money left over.[32] Elizabeth knighted Drake in April 1581, and in doing so she made it clear that she shared in his triumph and no longer cared to disguise the fact that she was all but at war with Spain.

But if Elizabeth gloried in Drake's achievement, Philip learned from him. He began to attempt to build fortifications at the Straits of Magellan and established a small fleet – the *Armada del Mar del Sur* – to protect the Pacific. Philip received a number of reports on what Drake had achieved; one of them noted that Drake's success came from the quality of the men whom he chose to work with him – that Drake himself was 'one of the finest sailors on the sea' and that he had a hand-picked crew – 'all men of an age and experience for war and each of them so experienced in it as if they were veterans of the Italian wars'.[33] Drake's return coincided with the climax of Pope Gregory's invasion fleet in Ireland. Some 800 men had actually been landed in Ireland, and if the English defenders managed to deal with them quickly enough – and to execute virtually all of them – Philip himself must have taken satisfaction from two achievements: the fleet had been commanded by a Spanish admiral – Juan Martínez de Recalde – and it had landed men on Elizabeth's soil.

4 War and Peace: 1580-1585

The death of King-Cardinal Henry of Portugal came at an auspicious time for Philip. He had made a truce with Ottoman Turkey in 1577 and the Sultan's commitments to war with Safavid Persia made it probable that the ceasefire in the Mediterranean would endure, at least in the immediate future. France was plunging ever deeper into the vortex of religious and civil war. Philip was able to plan the conquest of Portugal secure in the knowledge that he was unlikely to meet with opposition from his two major enemies. At the same time, the volume of treasure from the New World was increasing dramatically; in September 1580 nearly 15,000,000 ducats worth of silver were registered at Seville and a year later another 10,000,000 were recorded. In the years 1581-90 nearly twice as much silver was registered in Seville than in the previous decade.[1]

The acquisition of Portugal was of profound significance to Philip. He was himself half-Portuguese, and in bringing Portugal under his rule he would be paying homage to the memory of his beloved mother. It had long been an ambition of the Castilian crown to unify the kingdoms of Iberia under its own leadership, and the exotic riches of the Portuguese empire only made the prospect more enticing. For all these reasons, Philip prepared with special diligence for the unique opportunity that would come when Henry died.

The King-Cardinal expired in 1580. Philip proclaimed that he had been called by God to be king of Portugal and that anyone who resisted him would be punished as rebels. To add substance to this threat, he appointed the duke of Alba as general of the land forces to be employed in the annexation of Portugal; Alba's name alone would terrify many Portuguese. Álvaro de Bazán, Marquis of Santa Cruz was to command the naval forces that would be required to transport the army and to seal Portugal off from invasion. The Spanish expeditionary forces were very substantial indeed; Alba's army came to consist of 23,000 men and Santa Cruz's navy of ninety-nine galleys, thirty royal ships and sixty supply and support ships, as well as about 9,000 men.[2] Only one serious threat emerged to Philip's claim to the Portuguese crown: Dom Antonio, Prior of Crato and Sebastian's illegitimate cousin, declared his claim to the throne.

On 30 June Alba took the main body of his army into Portugal. There was no significant resistance as the Spanish troops worked their way methodically along the road to Lisbon, reducing one fortress after another. At the same time, Santa Cruz sailed from Puerto de Santa María to Setúbal. The two forces joined at Cascais at the end of July and Alba then led the army along the north bank of the Tagus to Lisbon. Antonio had managed to raise a force of some

10,000 men but it was distinguished by patriotism rather than by military discipline or leadership and it was no match for Alba and his veterans. The armies met on the outskirts of Lisbon on 25 August. Within hours, 3,000 of Antonio's troops were dead and the rest had fled. Antonio escaped into northern Portugal, where he tried to rally support. He had no success, and in May 1581 he sailed for France, never to return to Portugal.

Philip's conquest of Portugal was the high-point of his reign, and he luxuriated in it, joyously proclaiming that 'I inherited it, I bought it; I conquered it'.[3] It was a legitimate boast. The acquisition of a proud kingdom and its empire greatly added to his prestige. He acquired, too, the great harbour of Lisbon, defensible against the northerners and a watchtower over the Atlantic.

Philip and his court were based in Badajoz while the conquest was completed. The town did not have the facilities to accommodate the court and disease spread in the royal households. Philip himself was struck down and for a fortnight hovered at the point of death. But while he survived, his wife did not: Anna died on 26 October. Philip never remarried. In another way too the conquest of Portugal had proved expensive. Even the fabulous returns of American silver were not sufficient to cover Philip's expenditure in the early 1580s. Already by the spring of 1582 the maintenance of his armed forces in Portugal had cost some 2,500,000 ducats. Philip had to arrange new loans.[4]

When he met the Cortes of Portugal at Tomar, Philip received the homage of leading Portuguese and made a series of important promises about the continuing independence of his new realm – the kingdom would retain its own laws and coinage, the symbols of its independence; meetings of the cortes would not be held outside the kingdom; a council of Portugal would remain at his shoulder to represent the needs of the kingdom to him. In making his promises, Philip glossed over one of the harsh realities facing his new subjects – Portugal, its empire and its shipping would now attract the attentions of Philip's northern enemies. The Cortes concluded, on 29 May Philip formally entered Lisbon. He then set about establishing a government in the kingdom. There still remained much for Philip to do in Portugal when he heard of the death in Madrid of his heir, Diego Felix, from smallpox (21 November 1582). He was obliged now to return to Madrid. It took him some little time to make his dispositions and not until 11 February 1583 did he cross the frontier into Spain.

While Portugal had been annexed with relatively little difficulty, only two of the nine islands of the Azores accepted Philip's sovereignty and he had now to ensure that the others did so. The Azores stood at a strategic junction in the Atlantic; they welcomed the Portuguese galleons as they recovered from their exhausting journey round the Cape from Asia and they served, too, as a point of recovery and collection for the Spanish galleons carrying the silver of the New World before the dangerous last leg of their journey. But the islands extended across 400 miles of water and so were vulnerable to attack by French ships and even, indeed, by the English. Philip dared not allow the islands to fall within the orbit of France or England. The Azores had to be conquered

This would be no easy task. The islands stood 900 sea miles away from Iberia and stretched over 300 miles in length. For the first year of this campaign, Philip had to take a defensive posture. In the autumn of 1581 he despatched Don Pedro de Valdés, General of the Squadron of Galicia, to prevent Dom Antonio landing a fleet in the Azores. Valdés was the most fractious of Spain's naval commanders and perhaps also the most ambitious: he seems to have taken it upon himself to go beyond his orders and actually conquer the islands. He failed humiliatingly; on 25 July 1582 he landed 350 men on Terceira, but his troops were dispersed by the enemy driving a herd of bulls at them. They broke line and were massacred; only thirty escaped. Valdés himself on returning to Lisbon was arrested on a charge of dereliction of duty.[5]

Philip was as embarrassed as he was enraged by Valdés's failure. Soon he had cause for deep anxiety, for in February 1582 he learned that Filippo Strozzi, an Italian soldier of fortune who was related to Catherine de' Medici, was preparing a force in France with which to invade the Azores in support of Dom Antonio. Philip organized the first great Atlantic expedition of his reign to counter this menace. Naturally, he gave the command to Santa Cruz. The fleet comprised sixty-one ships and twenty-one galleys and was armed with 15,000 men. Santa Cruz was able to defeat Strozzi's force, but not without difficulty; 1,200 enemy were killed, Strozzi himself among them, and 500 prisoners were taken, including 100 Frenchmen of rank. Santa Cruz lost only 224 men. He executed all those of his captives who were over seventeen years of age. Philip thoroughly approved. He heard a celebratory mass in the cathedral at Lisbon and organized a splendid series of fireworks and celebrations to mark his victory.[6] But although the threat from France had receded, the Azores remained unconquered – an open opportunity to the enemies of Spain.

On 28 June 1583 Santa Cruz sailed out of Lisbon once again, this time to conquer the islands. He took with him a very substantial fleet – ninety-eight ships with a gross weight of 22,749 *toneladas* carried 15,372 soldiers, sailors and oarsmen. Part of the reason for the success of the campaign was the use of galleys and galleons in conjunction. The oared fighting craft ferried the soldiers to the shore and disembarked them with efficiency. The French were quickly routed. Once again, Santa Cruz administered brutal justice to his opponents; more than sixty Portuguese were hanged, and some of their bodies were then quartered as a terrible recognition of the price of rebellion.[7] For Philip himself, the victory was one of the high-points of his reign, ranking with the military triumphs at Malta and Lepanto, and he commemorated it on the walls of the Escorial.

The conquest of the Azores marked the end of Philip's use of galleys as the core of his fighting ships. He had employed ninety-nine galleys in the conquest of Portugal in 1580, twenty-one in the Azores in 1582 and only fourteen in the campaign of 1583. For the new warfare of the 1580s he needed galleons rather

The Conquest of the Azores, 1583.

than galleys. He had acquired twelve galleons – ten of them in prime condition – with the conquest of Portugal, and some thirty-five high-sided ships (albeit of indeterminate quality) in 1583. He now began the creation of what would become an Atlantic fleet. In 1576 Philip had established a fleet to protect the Indies run (the Armada de la Guarda de la Carrera de las Indias) and as soon as Portugal was secure he had Santa Cruz lead a commission to examine how to protect the carrera de las Indias and the Azores. The commission recommended that the Armada de la Guarda de la Carrera de las Indias should be strengthened. Philip agreed. In the years 1582-84, nine galleons were built in Santander and the construction of 15,000 tons of shipping was undertaken in Vizcaya. The Indies galleons were completed in 1584. Philip was at last, and with dramatic suddenness, developing the nucleus of an Atlantic fleet.[8]

Philip acknowledged Santa Cruz's achievements in Portugal and the Azores by raising him on 23 June 1584 to the offices of Captain General of the Atlantic Sea and Captain General of the Men of War of Portugal. When he swore the oaths to the two offices on 3 December 1584, Santa Cruz assumed control over Spain's Atlantic shipping and the defences of the coastline of Iberia and of the presidios in North Africa. But more than this, Philip also raised Santa Cruz to the grandeeship and to the position of Comendador Mayor de León in the Order of Santiago. This post went by tradition to the king's senior adviser.

Lisbon in the late sixteenth century.

Santa Cruz now had a unique status as the king's finest admiral and his most trusted confidant.[9] He arrived in Lisbon on 2 March 1585 and began working intensively to defend the coasts. His brother, Don Alonso de Bazán, reorganized the Galleys of Spain so that they could protect the south-west coast of Iberia and escort the treasure ships as they approached Cape St Vincent.[10] Lisbon was now the naval centre of the Atlantic fleet of the Spanish and Portuguese monarchy.

The conquests of Portugal and the Azores – and the comparative ease with which they had been accomplished – had profound strategic and indeed psychological consequences. It appeared that Philip was destined to succeed in all his military enterprises. Certainly, his two chief opponents – William of Orange and Elizabeth of England – realized now that they had to prepare their defences against the apparently irresistible growth in Spanish power.

Orange finally broke with his sovereign. In September 1580 he had the States General offer the throne of the Low Countries to the duke of Anjou, heir to the throne of Henry III, and in December he published his *Apologia* in which he savaged Philip as the murderer of his own son and a vindictive bigot devoid of moral scruple. More substantially, in the Hague on 26 July 1581, the representatives of the Union of Utrecht formally proclaimed the Edict of Abjuration, renouncing their loyalty to Philip and making the prince of Orange the count of Holland and Zeeland. The breach had been made.[11] Elizabeth, too, understood that she was at war in all but name: 'We think it good for the

King of Spain to be impeached both in Portugal and his Islands [i.e. the Azores] and also in the Low Countries, whereto we shall be ready to give such indirect assistance as shall not at once be a cause of war'.[12] When the duke of Anjou returned to the Low Countries in February 1582 to take the oath of allegiance to the States General, he was accompanied by the two leaders of the English war party, Sir Francis Walsingham and the earl of Leicester. The rebels needed all the help that they could find, for Parma was proving himself every bit as successful a general as Santa Cruz was an admiral; in 1582 he began the reconquest of Flanders and Brabant and in 1583 he took Dunkirk and Nieuport. These were not deep-water ports but their acquisition allowed Parma to re-establish a Spanish squadron in the North Sea.[13]

As Philip considered how best to develop the triumphs of Parma and Santa Cruz, he received a proposal to mount an 'Enterprise of England' from an Italian, Guiseppe Bastiani de Malatesti. Bastiani noted that the English were 'more disposed to infest others than to be infested themselves', and suggested that Philip should now turn his invincible forces on his northern foe.[14] More pertinently, from La Terceira on 9 August 1583 the Marquis of Santa Cruz wrote to Philip suggesting that he take action against Elizabeth, who had done 'so much harm to this kingdom'. God had given Philip great victories in the Azores and it was right that Philip should follow it up with an expedition against England, especially now that the new galleons were coming off the production line. Santa Cruz promised that he would make Philip king of England and that in doing so he would greatly ease the pressure on his territories in the Low Countries. Philip should bend the resources of his monarchy to make a concerted effort to raise the provisions and armaments necessary. Santa Cruz would himself come the Escorial to discuss the plan. He advised Philip that while the French might oppose the expedition, he himself had lost much respect for their fighting qualities in the campaigns in the Azores.[15]

When Philip returned to Madrid at the end of March 1583 he had been away for three years. He had developed an inner circle of advisers in Portugal: the Archduke Albert; Diego de Chaves, his confessor; Mateo Vázquez de Leca, Christovão de Moura and Juan de Idiáquez; Don Diego de Cabrera y Bobadilla, third count of Chinchón. They were now joined by Francisco Zapata de Cisneros, first count of Barajas, who was appointed to the presidency of the Council of Castile at the end of 1582 and by Juan de Zúñiga y Requesens, brother of Luis de Requesens, who returned to Madrid from Italy. These men were imperialists in foreign affairs and centralizers in domestic policy. They encouraged Philip in his growing conviction that he should pursue a more belligerent policy in northern Europe. Increasingly, they gave Philip the advice that he wanted to hear, urging him on to commit himself to the Enterprise of England.

Spanish power had been further augmented in the summer of 1584 by the deaths of William of Orange and the duke of Anjou. In truth, Anjou had not proved to be much of a leader. In January 1583 his troops had tried to storm Antwerp and been driven off ('the French Fury'), and in this retreat he lost whatever reputation as a general he had previously enjoyed. At the end of the year he left the Low Countries, already suffering from tuberculosis. He died on 10 June 1584. William of Orange was assassinated on 10 July by Baltasar Gerard. He died a national hero and throughout Europe the blame for his death was laid at Philip's door.[16]

The deaths of two of his major opponents brought immediate military and political advantages to Philip II. The death of Anjou promised additional political benefits, for he was the last of the sons of Henry II and the right of succession to the throne of France now passed to Henry, prince of Navarre. Henry appeared to have no great substance to him; he had abjured his religion on several occasions and was currently a Protestant. Nevertheless, the threat of a Protestant succession was a very serious one and the French Catholics organized to oppose it; on 31 January 1584 the Catholic League was re-established. It was led by the house of Guise and it rapidly became a nationwide organization. A few days later, a secret paramilitary organization came into being in Paris to protect Catholicism. 'The Sixteen' as it became known – because it represented the sixteen 'quarters' of the city – organized the city. Philip agreed to support the Catholic League with men and money, and thereby committed himself to becoming involved in the French civil and religious wars – and to do so while he was conducting a major war in the Low Countries and was beginning to seriously consider mounting an invasion of England.[17]

What propelled Philip to commit himself so deeply? Partly it was because he felt that Catholicism was on the defensive throughout western Europe. In England, Mary Stuart seemed only to be weakening Spain's position. In 1583 Ambassador Mendoza was implicated in a plot led by Nicholas Throckmorton to assassinate Elizabeth and replace her with Mary Stuart. He was expelled in January 1584. In 1585 William Parry was arrested and found to be carrying a letter from the pope's secretary approving his intention to assassinate Elizabeth (Popish plots were not distinguished by their originality). Even Burghley – the chief protagonist of the anti-war faction at court – was beginning to think that Spain's power might have to be opposed sooner rather than later. Elizabeth's income amounted to no more than one-tenth of what Philip received annually from the Indies alone: how long, Burghley wondered, would it be before Spain's power developed beyond the point where it could be restricted?[18]

As the situations in England, France and the Low Countries moved towards their separate but related crises, Philip had once again to abandon his capital to make an extended visit to his eastern kingdoms. He left Madrid on 19 January 1585 and was away until March 1586. While he was holding Cortes in Monzón, Philip himself fell seriously ill – once again a small town proved to be inadequate to house the royal court and its followers – and for two weeks (7-21 October) he was at the point of death. He made his confession but slowly he recovered his strength. For the second time in five years he had come close to death. Time was beginning to run out on him.[19]

Philip had to deal with two major crises while he was in Aragon. The first was in the great city of Naples, which came near to rebellion in protest at the fiscal demands of the crown. The threat was brutally crushed by the Viceroy, the duke of Osuna.[20] Less obviously threatening, but ultimately to be more damaging, was the final point of breakdown with England. In May 1585 Philip ordered the seizure of all northern ships in his ports in Spain and Portugal. It may well have been that he intended to strike primarily at the Dutch, who were blithely carrying on their trade with Spain while fighting a war with her and perhaps that he intended to warn Elizabeth about the costs to her of continuing her aid to the rebels. Whatever Philip's strategy, the affair was crassly handled. The commission given by Philip to his agents in the ports proclaimed that 'the ships were embargoed to serve the Spanish crown on a forthcoming expedition'. One English ship, the *Primrose*, was standing off Bilbao when the *corregidor* of the town boarded her to read the proclamation seizing the ship and its cargo. Called upon to surrender, the crew seized the unfortunate *corregidor* and fled back to England with both him and his proclamation.[21] Philip's conduct particularly outraged the English merchant community because many of the ships had travelled to Spain to bring grain to alleviate food shortages and, moreover, had done so with Philip's guarantee of their safe conduct. The news of Spanish perfidy – and the publication of Philip's proclamation – aroused widespread fury, especially in London; the city offered, perhaps over-grandly, to fit out seven score ships to take revenge on Spain. Elizabeth's response was to the point; on 1 July Francis Drake was commissioned to sail to Vigo to negotiate for the return of the ships. No one seriously thought of Drake as a diplomat, and in fact his mission had been planned before the seizure of the English ships. Philip's actions merely provided the justification for a mission, the real purpose of which was to inflict as much damage as possible on Spain's defences.[22]

A further step on the road to war came with the election of Felice Peretti as Pope Sixtus V on 24 April 1585. Sixtus was determined that his pontificate would be marked by a triumph against the enemies of the Faith. Among his many projects, Sixtus wanted to remove Elizabeth from the English throne. At the end of 1585 Pope Sixtus therefore renewed the *cruzada* tax for seven years to help Philip to fund the 'Enterprise of England'. Philip thought this woefully inadequate.[23] Sixtus was also determined to prevent the accession of Henry of Navarre to the French throne and so on 9 September 1585 he excommunicated Henry, thereby prohibiting Catholics from accepting him as king of France. His actions brought on another war of religion in France. It was fought between King Henry III, Henry of Guise and Henry of Navarre and became known as the 'War of the Three Henries'. A Catholic crusade had come about to prevent the accession of Henry of Navarre to the French throne and it seemed only to be the first part of a European-wide crusade led by the pope.

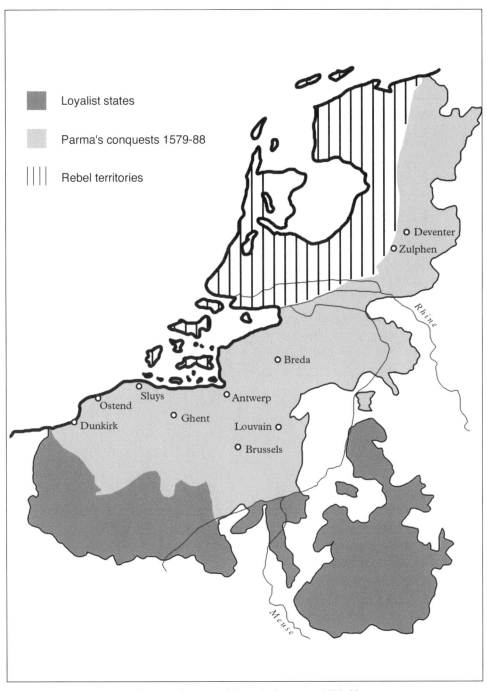

Loyalist states

Parma's conquests 1579-88

Rebel territories

Deventer
Zulphen
Rhine
Breda
Sluys
Ostend
Antwerp
Dunkirk
Ghent
Louvain
Brussels
Meuse

The Low Countries: 2 Parma's Conquests, 1579-88

As Sixtus brought the power and influence of the papacy to bear to bring about a Catholic crusade in western Europe, the duke of Parma thrust all before him in the Low Countries. In 1583 he captured the Channel ports of Dunkirk and Nieuport and in 1584-85 he followed this up by conquering one great city after another in the Low Countries – Brussels in March 1584; Bruges in April; Ghent in September. The greatest triumph of all came when on 17 August 1585 Antwerp surrendered to him.

The conquest of Antwerp was one of the great military achievements of the sixteenth century. Parma laid siege to the city by constructing a fortified bridge across the Scheldt to cut the great city off from the sea. The construction of the bridge was a thing of wonder, needing more than 10,000 tree trunks and thirty-two hulks. It was completed in February 1585. On 5 April the defenders of Antwerp made a desperate attempt to lift the siege by attacking the bridge with four fireships – named 'Gambetti's hellburners' after their inventor – and thirteen support ships. They cut into the bridge but did not breach it. 'The hellships of Antwerp' did however kill some 800 men and created an enduring terror among Parma's troops; those who had seen the hellships did not forget them. On 27 August Parma entered the city. In three years he had doubled the area of the Low Countries controlled by Spain. Philip heard about the capture of Antwerp in the middle of the night and rushed to Isabella's room shouting 'Antwerp is ours'. The triumph at Antwerp seemed to be the expression of Philip's irresistible power.[24]

Even before Antwerp fell, Elizabeth had reached the conclusion that she had to assist the Dutch and on 20 August 1585 she agreed to the Treaty of Nonsuch with the United Provinces. She undertook to provide 4,000 infantry and 400 cavalry to save Antwerp, to pay 600,000 florins a year and to send a naval expedition to the Indies to distract Philip. Elizabeth justified herself to Europe for helping rebels against a lawful monarch and in the 'Declaration of Richmond' (11 October 1585) she insisted that Philip had ignored her attempts at mediation and had also supported an expedition against her in Ireland and had connived in attempts to assassinate her. At the turn of the year the earl of Leicester arrived in the Low Countries to command the English troops; there were by now some 8,000 of them.[25] Elizabeth had crossed the line dividing war and peace with the king of Spain.

As a first retaliatory step, Elizabeth had her government issue letters of marque making it lawful for merchants and others who had had their goods or ships seized 'to set upon by force of arms, and to take and apprehend upon the seas, any of the ships or goods of the subjects of the king of Spain in as ample and full manner as if it were in the time of open war between her Majesty and the said King of Spain'.[26] As a second step, Elizabeth charged her greatest sea captain to exact revenge for her; Sir Francis Drake sailed on 14 September 1585 with twenty-nine ships which included two of Elizabeth's prize ships (the *Elizabeth Bonaventure* and the *Aid*) and Leicester's *Galleon Leicester*. Drake also took with him 2,300 infantry. He left to a tumultuous send-off, with scenes of

The bridge at Antwerp (above) and the attack on it (below).
On 5 April 1585 seventeen ships attacked the bridge in an attempt to break it. Four of them were 'hellburners',
packed with explosives under the direction of the Italian engineer Gambelli. Hundreds of Spaniards were killed
and Parma himself was injured but the bridge held. Antwerp surrendered four months later.
Parma appeared now to be invincible.

Sir Francis Drake (1543-96).

'great jollity'. He stopped off at Vigo to see if he could find any ships (or captive Englishmen) but found nothing much and spent a fortnight plundering the town and its hinterland. He did no great harm but the insult to the king of Spain was manifest and Drake drove it home by despoiling some churches. He then moved on to the Cape Verde Islands, where he took on provisions for the Atlantic crossing. By Christmas he was in the Caribbean and at the very turn of the year – by the English calendar – he captured Santo Domingo. It was a poor town and yielded little. After a month during which he repaired his ships and took on provisions, Drake moved on to the great port of Cartagena. He astonished the defenders by storming the bastions, and then agreed to accept a bribe not to destroy the town in its entirety. Drake then narrowly missed the treasure fleet returning to Spain. He made for home through the Bermuda Channel and, in another measured insult to Philip, destroyed the fort at San Agustín that had been the first Spanish settlement on the North American continent. He travelled north to Roanoke Island and rescued the starving English settlers there before returning home.[27]

Philip heard of Drake's exploits in early December. At this point he was pondering on a letter from Parma insisting that English assistance to the Dutch rebels was making them more determined to fight on.[28] Soon afterwards he received a letter from Juan Bautista de Tassis in Namur which noted that English help was bolstering the Protestant cause in France and recommended that an expedition be mounted against England. Knowing his sovereign, Tassis hinted that the queen of England was endeavouring to make herself the ruler of some of the patrimonial lands of the House of Burgundy.[29] Nothing could have been better calculated to stir Philip to make the commitment to the 'Enterprise of England.'

While Philip was discreet in his public utterances, senior ministers exploded in wrath. It was reported to London that the news of Drake's exploits created outrage; the Council of State was said to be 'much out of tune' when they heard of his activities and Juan de Idiáquez and the Count of Barajas (President of the Council of Castile) spoke angrily of what was being planned – and they 'did demand whether the Queen's Majesty of England did know the King of Spain's forces, and whether it made not her and her people to quake?'[30]

It is interesting that both Elizabeth and Philip understood and justified their respective positions by fundamentally defensive rationale. The Spanish perspective can be taken from an extraordinary document detailing the deliberations of Philip's Council of State. On 20 January 1588 – we shall have to jump ahead of the narrative briefly – the Spanish Council of State met to decide whether or not to recommend to the king that the fleet should sail against England. It concluded that the Enterprise should go ahead in the hope that God would favour it as His own cause. It was certainly the only way to secure the Indies trade, to free the Iberian coasts from English attacks and to cut out the English support to the rebels in the Low Countries. The view that the council presented to Philip was that the campaign against England was being fought for defensive reasons, to stop the English from helping the Dutch and from attacking Iberia itself and the Indies. The Dutch had resisted Spain for too long and it had cost Spain too much to fight them on land; if English assistance was cut off the revolt would wither.[31]

There does not appear to have been an equivalent document in the English archives detailing Elizabeth's reasoning. However, it is not difficult to discern her motivation. Since her accession to the throne, Philip II's enemies had been systematically weakened. The Turk had withdrawn from the Mediterranean; France had collapsed; Dom Antonio had been routed and exiled; William of Orange and Anjou were nearly four years in their graves; Philip's hegemony in Italy was unchallenged, and indeed a number of popes – traditionally a bulwark to Habsburg influence in the peninsula – had systematically supported his war efforts. The enormous empire of the kingdom of Portugal had been incorporated into the Spanish monarchy. The Catholic King's income had increased propitiously, the pirates rarely being able to penetrate the highly effective convoy system set up by Philip in the 1560s. True, the revolt of the Netherlands had proven to be a massive drain of resources and men. Yet Parma had proven one of the finest military commanders of his age; the capture of Antwerp made it clear that Philip's intention of re-conquering the provinces was a military possibility. Since 1577 Philip had been developing an Atlantic fleet. In comparison with the situation in 1559 – or, to add a historical perspective, at the outbreak of the Thirty Year's War in 1618 – the position of Spain among the Christian powers was that of unparalleled hegemony. Elizabeth signed a treaty with the rebellious Dutch provinces. From 1585 she would systematically support Philip II's rebels.

It should be clear that Elizabeth and Philip had consistently attempted to avoid full-scale warfare. Paradoxically, the very means by which they had hoped to avoid this had, by late 1585, brought them to the point of no return. The extraordinary prowess of their commanders – and in particular of Drake, Santa Cruz and Parma – had made direct conflict inevitable. The differing motivations pushing Elizabeth and Philip to warfare were, therefore, of great importance. Elizabeth went to war because she feared that not to do so might cost her everything; Philip went to war because, in the medium term at least, peace had become more expensive than war.

5 Plans, Preparations and Providence

On 29 December 1585 Philip informed Parma that he had decided to proceed to 'the chief business' (*el negocio principal*). This statement needed no further clarification. *El negocio principal* had assumed a special meaning in governmental circles over the two previous decades: it referred to a military solution for the problem of Elizabeth Tudor. Philip reminded Parma that 'without a port nothing can be done'. By that he meant a deep-water port.[1]

Having made the political decision that he had to proceed with the Enterprise of England, Philip plunged into an exhaustive investigation of the historical methods employed in the nine seaborne invasions of the British Isles since 1066. He also devoted himself to the study of the geography of British coastal regions.[2] The Spanish government believed that Philip could draw upon forces and resources far larger than those mobilized by Elizabeth, and that the capture of London had to be the principal military objective of the attack. Philip invited his most trusted commanders to propose how this might be achieved. Three clear strategies emerged. The first was based upon the premise that Elizabeth's fleet had to be prevented from opposing the Spanish invasion force. It proposed a diversionary raid somewhere in the British isles, probably in Ireland, which would occupy Elizabeth's fleet and allow the main invasion force to cross the Channel and disembark unopposed. The second plan was based on surprise, and was founded upon Parma's calculation that the sailing time from Dunkirk to Margate was twelve hours without a following wind, and only eight hours with one. This would allow the Army of Flanders to make it across the Channel unopposed. Since the soldiers could be placed into barges in around 36 hours, all that was required was favourable weather conditions. Within two days of the commencement of the operation, Parma's troops might be disembarking on the English coast. It would be profoundly difficult for Elizabeth to respond to this threat. However, this strategy involved a high degree of risk, as the lack of a deep-water port in the regions of the Netherlands controlled by the Spanish would mean that Parma's men would have to cross the Channel in flat-bottomed craft or barges which would be vulnerable to high seas and to attack from the Dutch and English fleets. The third plan, advocated by Santa Cruz, proposed that Philip should send an invincible fleet from Spain against England. The attraction of this plan was its simplicity: the invasion force would command overwhelming power; the English would be unable to oppose its inexorable progress towards their coast; it could disembark infantry at or near London.

Philip settled upon a scheme which was basically an amalgamation of these strategies. Essentially the plan eventually decided upon was for a fleet to sail from Spain and Portugal, to collect the Army of Flanders (embarked upon barges) from Dunkirk and then escort Parma and his men across the Channel. The Armada would then guard the seas in order to prevent relief reaching London. England would be isolated from the continent. Its essential function having been served, the Armada might then attack an area known to contain a large Catholic population, most probably in Ireland.

Essentially Philip and his ministers envisaged two possible successful outcomes. The first, the best-case scenario, involved a full-scale invasion of southern England led by Parma with the intention of capturing London, preferably with Elizabeth and her court still in it. The second depended upon capturing a position – perhaps the Isle of Wight – which could be fortified and defended, thus forcing a cowered Elizabeth to the negotiating table. Historians have long suspected that this second eventuality was as much as Philip could realistically expect to achieve. According to this point of view, his intention was to neutralize Elizabeth rather than eliminate her.

Whatever the ultimate intention of Philip II, four major areas of military strategy emerge from the events of 1587-8. First, both sides sought to gain the initiative by carrying out their strategic objectives early in the season or before the enemy could respond. In the English case, this entailed pre-emptive raids on Cadiz, Coruña or Lisbon designed to destroy the preparations before the Armada could even leave port. Second, the size of the fleets, the number of men garrisoning them and the extended period of action (six months was the provisional time-span for the Armada campaign) brought major operational and logistical problems; this was not only because provisions had to be brought and preserved, but also because it was essential that the commanders knew how much longer they could afford to be at sea. Third, the relative qualities of the Spanish and English ships, guns, commanders and soldiers played a highly significant role. Fourth, the Enterprise of England depended upon the two commanders maintaining excellent communication with one another. Success relied upon the Armada being able to join with and escort the transport ships carrying the army of Flanders; in order for the fleet to be able to do this, the two commanders would have to coordinate their actions very closely.

Commanders such as Santa Cruz had gained their experience of warfare in the Mediterranean – a theatre of conflict in which the logistical limitations of the crafts employed played a very major role. Although in fact the question of logistics did not determine the outcome of the campaign in 1588, in differing circumstances the question of food, wine and water might have been the difference between victory and defeat. Had the Armada not been forced into the North Sea, then the amount of food and drink available to the two fleets would have become the crucial determinant of how long each could remain at sea. In the event of a successful disembarkation in England, the movement and objectives of Parma's army would have been determined in part by its need to feed itself. It is not surprising, therefore, that the duke of Medina Sidonia (who replaced Santa Cruz, who died in February 1588) laid down precise instructions to his officials, even detailing the order in which provisions should be consumed. The detailed auditing of provisions aboard the Armada had one concrete beneficial consequence: the captain-general of the fleet reduced the daily rations fed to each man as the fleet embarked on its precarious tour of Scotland and Ireland; had he not done so, it is possible that the men would have starved. It can also be surmised that the decision to sail around Scotland and Ireland may in part have been motivated by the realization that the fleet had just over one month's provisions – enough to last until around mid-September. Related to this point were considerations of health: disease could destroy a fleet more effectively than any human enemy. Outbreaks of plague or fever had to be closely monitored and isolated.

An essential component of many of the plans for attack and counter-attack involved mobilizing a fleet or squadron in order to sail very early in the campaigning season. For instance, Philip II ordered Medina Sidonia to sail in January 1588 when it appeared that it might be possible to catch the English unprepared. This, however, proved impossible. One of the features of the years 1587-8 was the frequency with which expeditions were delayed or seriously complicated by poor weather. By all reckoning, the Enterprise of England should have been undertaken in 1587; as we shall see, the combined agencies of Drake and the elements brought about the postponement. Still, Philip expected to see the Armada sail in the winter of 1587-8 in order to take the English unawares. Both sides sought to gather and analyse reports on the preparations and intentions of the other. By the time that the Armada finally reached England, Elizabeth's government had made enormous progress in preparing her fleet and militia.

The third point of major interpretative importance concerned the relative merits of the ships, mariners and guns of the respective navies. A great deal of valuable research has been done into this subject. It is generally agreed that the English fighting ships – the dreadnoughts – were lighter, swifter and more manoeuvrable than their direct adversaries, the Spanish and Portuguese galleons. It is also agreed that Elizabeth's ships had developed a form of gun carriage and a technique which allowed them to discharge and reload their ordnance more rapidly than the Spanish could do. This was partly because Elizabeth's navy carried more guns and gunners than did their adversaries. The Spanish ships had less than one-third of the long-range guns that the English had (172:497) and only half of the heavy and medium guns (165:251). In all, it has been calculated that the Spanish firepower was equivalent to three-quarters of that of the English, and it may have been much less. Indeed, the Spanish fleet was carrying only three times as much gunpowder as Santa Cruz had used in a single day's combat in the Azores in 1583.[3] But it was also because the Spanish had yet to realize the full strategic value of artillery fire. Medina Sidonia in fact instructed the infantry aboard the Armada to abandon the guns and prepare to board the enemy as soon as battle was begun. At the Straits of Dover the Armada was out-sailed and it was out-gunned.

The two fleets employed differing offensive strategies which were determined by the capabilities of their ships and artillery. The bulkier Spanish vessels' favoured means of attacking enemy craft was by grappling – in other words by launching boarding raids involving hand-to-hand fighting. The English relied upon ordnance and rapid fire at a distance of less than 500yds. This gave an advantage to the English, since the speed and mobility of their craft allowed them to stay at a distance from the enemy and therefore prevent the Spanish from boarding. The Armada sought to negate the English advantages by maintaining a defensive crescent formation, and this strategy was very successful.

The superiority of Elizabeth's navy over Philip's Armada has traditionally dominated the analysis of the campaign of 1588. To suggest that the relative quality of the fleets, their guns and mariners was only one of three or four general points of roughly equal importance in 1588 constitutes, therefore, a revision of some importance. However, this contention can be justified on a number of grounds. First, it would be wrong to think that one armada fought the other. In reality, only select bands of excellent vessels on each side were expected to engage the enemy. Perhaps as few as forty vessels were actively involved in the fighting. These ships were vital to the success of the strategies: as we shall see, when a number of the best of Philip II's men-of-war were briefly scattered from the armada in a storm off Coruña in late June, nearly all the commanders thought that there was no point in proceeding with the expedition. Second, the actual details of the fighting do not support the contention that one side decisively defeated the other in combat. In comparison with the battle of Lepanto, fought seventeen years previously, the outcome of the confrontation off Gravelines was highly ambiguous; for a moment the Spanish actually thought that their fleet had emerged victorious from the confrontation. Third, the plan as developed by Medina Sidonia and Philip did not depend upon the defeat of the enemy at sea; it was only the catastrophic decision to drop anchor at Calais and the effect of the fireships which brought about a general engagement. Of course, it is very revealing that the English should choose to scatter and fight the enemy: clearly these were circumstances in which they felt confident that they held the advantage. Conversely, the Armada was invincible as long as it maintained its discipline. Yet the details of the fifteen years of warfare between England and Spain after 1588 do not support the contention that the English had developed a vastly advanced design of ship and a superior level of seamanship and gunnery.

In explicitly referring to the campaign against Elizabeth of England as God's design, Philip II and his advisors were consciously expressing the religious piety of the day. Great victories were celebrated as an expression of Catholic piety; defeat was attributed to a divine punishment for the sins of the community. In part, this was a rhetorical device of the sort commonly employed in early modern Europe. But behind it lay genuine beliefs, and ones shared by the most intelligent and experienced military commanders of the day. This was because Providence really did hold the key to the success and failure of campaigns. In naval expeditions, the winds were often the most significant manifestation of His desire: they allowed ships to sally from port, they dispersed, delayed, stranded or rescued fleets at decisive moments. The Almighty might intervene in a number of differing ways – through an outbreak of disease or through cloudless nights. The descent of fog or mists, for example, might be of enormous importance, as had been the case at Malta in 1565 when unusual mists allowed a company of Spaniards to reach the besieged Christian garrison. This brought a strange mental flexibility: setbacks could always be re-interpreted. As we shall see, Philip II and Medina Sidonia were capable of assessing and re-assessing events with little or no difficulty. As they strove to discern God's will, men on both sides were forced to face the psychological burden that any given event was an indication of Providence. There was always scope for a certain amount of reinterpretation, but in the end defeat in battle had to be accepted as divine punishment. This was a burden which sat heavily on the men and women of the sixteenth century.

This is important in understanding the code of piety and proper behaviour, as well as the sense of crusade, which the commanders on both sides sought to impart to their men. In his instructions to Medina Sidonia, Philip claimed that he had to prepare the Armada 'in the service of our Lord' and recognize that 'all victories are the gifts of God Almighty'. Medina Sidonia's instructions to the fleet were similar. The chief purpose of the enterprise was, he insisted, the king's desire to serve God and to convert England to the Catholic faith. Accordingly, prayers were to be said daily and everyone on the fleet was to be confessed before departure. Both the king and the admiral stressed that there was to be no conduct on board which might offend the Almighty – no swearing or blaspheming – and no gambling, which might lead to disturbances.

It should also be said that a military undertaking of the size and complexity of the Enterprise of England had rarely been made, although Philip and his advisors studied history to see what could be learnt. Yet previous invasions launched from the continent could not be compared to the unique circumstances in which Philip, Medina Sidonia and Parma made their plans. In short, nobody could be certain of the outcome or even of the chances of success. As we shall see, Medina Sidonia changed his mind on at least three occasions, oscillating between genuine optimism and unchecked pessimism. Parma did so twice. One of the consequences of this uncertainty was that both commanders were careful to spell out problems in the plan; these served essentially as excuses in case of eventual failure, although, again, such pronouncements were rhetorical devices commonly employed in early modern Europe by military commanders faced with an exacting political master and a complex military operation. The English also wavered; many were profoundly impressed by the scale of the Spanish preparations. It appears

Elizabeth would have accepted peace terms had acceptable ones been offered to her. Philip's reasoning for believing that the cost of peace with Elizabeth was exorbitant can in part be understood by the fact that he had fought the Ottoman Turk in the Mediterranean with funds provided directly or indirectly by Rome. On 2 January 1586 he wrote to his ambassador in Rome, the Count of Olivares. He reminded Olivares of the pope's insistence that he undertake the Enterprise of England but claimed that he could not commit himself to do so until he received solid financial support from the papacy. He stressed that the reason for sending the fleet had to be to reduce England to obedience to the Roman Church and to put Mary Stuart on the throne.

This was not entirely true. Philip had always had misgivings about putting Mary in the throne of England on account of her links with the French court. These had been augmented by the concern that if Mary died her son James would inherit her claim on the throne, and since 1582 he had been surrounded by a Protestant clique. Since both Mary and James presented profoundly problematic alternatives to Elizabeth Tudor, Philip entered into negotiation with Sixtus hoping to have his daughter Isabella succeed to the throne of England.[4] Sixtus was not going to open the coffers before he was certain of Philip's intentions. Finally, in the spring of 1587, realizing that the Enterprise of England would undoubtedly now go ahead, Pope Sixtus agreed to deposit 1,000,000 ducats against the expenses of the fleet. Having accepted the papal subsidy, Philip had to put up with the irritation of papal suspicion that he would pocket the money and negotiate terms with Elizabeth. In turn, Olivares conjectured that Sixtus was really searching for ways of avoiding making the down-payment to Madrid.[5]

Exactly as Philip was finalizing his plans for the Enterprise of England, Mary Stuart had some letters smuggled out of her prison. Walsingham had access to her letters (and may even have invented the whole procedure) and in June 1586 read with the very keenest of interest a letter from Mary inviting a French or Spanish invasion to place her on the throne of England. Mary also gave approval to a plot led by Anthony Babington to assassinate Elizabeth. In her own hand, Mary provided the evidence that would send her to the block. She was put on trial in October 1586 and found guilty of treason. Elizabeth agonized over whether to execute Mary and prevaricated time and again about signing the warrant, but eventually she did so. Mary Stuart was beheaded on 18 February 1587. Philip was genuinely sympathetic to Mary, but understood that her death served his political purposes for it removed the threat of a Franco-Scottish succession to the English throne, freeing him of the fear that his armada might succeed in eliminating Elizabeth only to replace her with the pro-French Mary Stuart.

In France events conspired to advance Philip's cause. During the night of 11-12 May 1588, Henry III had fifteen detachments of Swiss and French troops take up position at key points throughout the city. On the morning of 12 May, Paris found itself an occupied city. But the 'Sixteen' had anticipated his actions and with mysterious efficiency they had barriers thrown up in the streets of each of their districts. The king and his army were immobilized and on 13 May Henry sneaked out of his capital. He would not now be able to give any significant aid to Elizabeth.[6]

The diplomatic situation across Europe in the years 1586-8 favoured Philip and his armada. On 26 January 1586, Philip wrote from San Lorenzo to the Marquis of Santa Cruz, ordering him to establish 'a good fleet' in Lisbon for action by the end of April or – at the very latest – the beginning of May. The damage done to shipping by English and other corsairs had now to be dealt with. The new fleet was ostensibly to operate along the Atlantic coast of Iberia and to stop corsair attacks, but both king and admiral knew that it had another purpose. The planning had begun for the Enterprise of England.[7] Again, news of the preparations found their way quickly back to England; on 14 February a William Melsam, who had been a prisoner of the Inquisition, reported to the Privy Council that 'the King of Spain prepareth a great Army and Navy, as well of galleys as of ships… they do give out speech that they do mean for to land in the Isle of Wight 50,000 men, more 50,000 men into Ireland, 50,000 men also in the backside of Scotland'.[8] It was remarkable that news travelled so fast. Elizabeth was as well informed as Philip and his ministers of what was happening. Planning proceeded quickly; on 2 April Bautista de Tassis insisted that Flanders should be the base for the invasion, and on 20 April Parma despatched to Philip his own plan for the invasion of England.[9]

Philip now appointed the men who would work with Santa Cruz in preparing the fleet. Don Agustín de Mexía was named as *maestre de campo* of the infantry raised in Andalusia. Mexía was one of Spain's senior soldiers with extensive service in Flanders. Pedro Coco Calderón was appointed as accountant of the fleet and two secretaries were named for the Council of War – Don Andrés de Alva to deal with the papers of the Sea and Don Andrés de Prada as Secretary for Land Affairs. Detailed reports were commissioned regarding the ports of England and Ireland and of the cost of maintaining the forces that would be needed for the Enterprise for a full year.[10]

Elizabeth, too, knew that now it was only a question of time before Philip sent his fleet against her and so she responded in her traditional manner: on 12 April 1587 – very early in the campaigning season – Drake left Plymouth with a royal commission instructing him to do as much damage as he could to Spanish preparations. He commanded a fleet of sixteen warships which included four of Elizabeth's own galleons. Drake followed the spirit of his instructions to the letter – a novelty for him. He arrived off Cadiz on 29 April to find sixty Spanish ships at anchor. He sailed straight into the harbour and destroyed twenty large vessels (although characteristically he claimed credit for having sent over thirty to the bottom). News of his arrival promptly reached Seville and on 30 April the duke of Medina Sidonia hurried with the militia to relieve Cadiz. He sent fireships against the English flotilla but they inflicted little damage, and the English were able to escape unharmed. The size of the preparations had, however, profoundly impressed the intruders. Drake reported to Walsingham that 'the like preparation was never heard of nor known as the King of Spain hath and daily maketh to invade England'. In a carefully considered postscript he urged Walsingham that 'I dare not almost write unto your honour of the great forces we hear the King of Spain hath out in the Straits. Prepare in England strongly, and most by sea. Stop him now, and stop him ever. Look well to the coast of Sussex'.[11]

From Cadiz, Drake sailed to Sagres, where he captured the castle and used the harbour as a base from which he destroyed forty-seven small cargo vessels. He created terror along the coast, and Spanish and Portuguese shipping came to a halt. When Drake heard that a large Portuguese carrack – the *São Phelipe* – was headed with a cargo of treasure and jewels for the Azores, he pursued it and captured it as once he had the *Cacafuego*. When he reached Plymouth (6 July 1587) he brought with him a great deal of Philip's treasure and the knowledge that he had severely damaged the preparations for the Armada. He had almost brought the Indies trade to a halt; in 1586 a record 148 ships had crossed from Cadiz to the Indies, but in 1587 only thirty-one did so. Moreover, Drake had inadvertently caused profound damage to the fleet that Philip had been so laboriously collecting in Lisbon, for Santa Cruz sailed from Lisbon on 16 July with thirty ships to protect the Azores and the *carrera de Indias* against Drake. He spent three months at sea and when he returned to Lisbon on 29 September his ships were badly in need of repair and many of his men were weakened by the long voyage.[12] And his instructions were waiting for him for the Enterprise of England. They were dated 14 September 1587.[13]

These instructions were the fruit of Philip's long and deep commitment and meditation upon what could be achieved. But they were also muddled; Philip had sought to resolve the contradictions implicit in the plans presented by Parma and Santa Cruz by merging them. He thereby made a hotchpotch of a plan that could not really work. The two prescriptions that Philip himself had laid down in December 1585 were not followed through – there was no deepwater port and there most certainly was no secrecy now about his intentions. He had decided that Santa Cruz should sail up the Channel to meet the Army of Flanders and transport its elite troops across to 'the Cape of Margate'. The army would then march on London where it would win a position from which negotiations could be carried out. It was not stated how the troops were to be taken on board with the English fleet at hand or indeed with the Dutch cromsters able themselves to prevent Parma's troops sailing out to the galleons on their small flat-bottomed troop-carriers. But for Santa Cruz the plan was a desperate disappointment, for he was ordered to play what he considered to be a subordinate role; his would not be the glory of conquest but merely the service of troop-carrier. He was ordered not to engage the English fleet but to have as his sole purpose the junction with and the transport of Parma's troops. For a man with Santa Cruz's unrivalled success in war this was humiliation indeed and he appears to have seriously considered resignation.[14]

The capture of Sluys.

The Army of Flanders demonstrated the full range of its abilities in the capture of Sluys (in 1587). With the capture of the town, Parma appeared to complete his control of the coast from which his troops would embark on the Armada.

But for Philip himself there could now be nothing but action. So insistent was he that Santa Cruz should sail at once that the Marquis felt obliged to defend his honour. He pointed out that the fleet had to be repaired after its three months' voyage. Those repairs were duly carried out when on 16 November a violent storm hit Lisbon and damaged thirty-nine ships, some of them seriously. A further delay would take the earliest time of departure into December – and it was of course a thing unheard of for a great fleet to go to sea so late in the year.

Nevertheless it appeared that this most remarkable of fleets was going to do so. On 2 December, Santa Cruz held a general muster. He established that there were 16,260 sailors in Lisbon but that 1,100 (7%) of them were ill. Ten days later he wrote to Philip that the fleet might be able to sail in a month's time. But he himself was very unwell; he informed that he would prepare the fleet 'as long as life remains to me'. On 18 January Philip ordered him to go to sea without wasting a single hour. He insisted that 'our Armada will be superior in strength' to the English.[15] Santa Cruz was only to fight if he needed to ensure that Parma could cross to England: if the crossing could be effected without an engagement, so much the better. It was also likely that the Armada would have to engage a Dutch flotilla near the shore.

The Spanish sought to sail in winter. The English had to respond in kind. On 2 January – at a point in the year at which few would dare to venture to sea

Charles Howard, lord of Effingham (1536-1624).

Opposite page: Robert Dudley, earl of Leicester (1532-88).

– Elizabeth's Lord Admiral embarked at Rochester. Lord Howard had twenty-six royal ships under his command. It was intended that Drake should take five of these vessels as the core of a fleet of forty-or-so sail to burn as many of the Armada ships as he could. But gales prevented Drake from leaving harbour. There was much exaggeration about the number of royal ships, but it is believed that they numbered sixty-eight, with fifteen private ships. As Howard went to Rochester the passport arrived from Parma for the peace commissioners to cross to the Low Countries. Leicester and Walsingham argued strongly in council that Parma was merely playing for time and had no serious interest in negotiations. But Elizabeth was determined to pursue every avenue for peace – or perhaps to while away every day that was possible. She let it be known that she was determined to make peace with Spain. She feared that if she lost her ships she would lose her kingdom. She also spoke scathingly of Drake – that he had never fought in a real battle and that the damage he had inflicted upon the enemy had served only to stir up Philip's anger against her![16]

As the Spanish Council of State conferred its blessing upon the Enterprise of England, on 31 January 1588 Parma wrote an extraordinary letter to Philip defending himself against what he took to be a suggestion by the king that he had not prepared as energetically as he might have done. Parma wrote with restrained but pointed fury. He insisted that his boats would not be capable of fighting their way out of port let alone crossing the Channel in the face of enemy ships. He reminded Philip that the repeated delays had undermined his preparations and that even now he did not have enough Spanish troops for his purposes. He insisted that Santa Cruz leave at once and went almost so far as to dissociate himself from the Enterprise of England: 'I now see that everything has turned out the reverse of what I expected and hoped. Secrecy, which was of the utmost importance, has not been maintained; and from Spain, Italy, and all parts come, not only news of the expedition, but full details of it'. His own preparations, while not perfect, were quite adequate. Stingingly, he reminded Philip that he had expected Santa Cruz in September and had hurried his men to the port: 'If the Marquis had come then, the crossing would have been easily effected with God's help', because the rebels and the English had not been ready to oppose him. He asserted again that he had 'carried out orders and served your Majesty with my invariable loyalty, exactitude and affection in this matter'. If Philip had ordered him to cross without Santa Cruz he would have done so. He was very hurt by Philip's rebuke and insisted that the delay in the arrival of the Armada was ruining the loyalist provinces of the Low Countries as well as the plans for the Enterprise of England itself. The burden of preparations could not be borne for much longer.[17] On the same day Parma also wrote to Philip that he believed that Elizabeth truly hoped for peace – that her fear of the Armada was genuine, not the least because of the expense incurred in defending her coastlines. Once negotiations opened he would find out for certain what the Queen's intentions were.[18] What the letters of 31 January showed – and recorded

Sir Martin Frobisher (1539-94).

Sir Walter Raleigh (1554-1618).

formally and carefully for the historical record – was that the duke of Parma had little or no confidence in the Enterprise of England and that he wanted to be rid of it.

Angry as he was, Parma retained his health. Philip and Santa Cruz were both crumbling under the strain of the long preparations and delays. Philip collapsed at Christmas and was confined to bed for a month. Santa Cruz contracted exanthematic fever, almost certainly due to visiting his men in hospital. On 9 February 1588, he died. Philip confessed himself grateful – perhaps none too tactfully – that his commander had died before the Enterprise set sail rather than after it had done so. He did, however, write courteously to the Marquis's kinsmen before turning his mind to finding another commander.[19]

He settled upon Alonso Pérez de Guzmán, seventh duke of Medina Sidonia, a supreme administrator but an inexperienced seafarer and a very reluctant commander of the fleet. Even while Medina Sidonia was being forced to accept command of the Armada, the duke of Parma was expecting the arrival of the fleet off the Low Countries. On 22 February 1588, five days after Medina Sidonia arrived in Lisbon, Parma wrote to Philip informing him that he had loaded the munitions on board ship and collected the transport boats at Dunkirk to await the embarkation of the troops. However, Parma had to admit that the number of men under his command was shrinking alarmingly because of their exposure to the elements; he had now only 18,000 men. By 20 March Parma was writing of the 'lamentable and astonishing mortality amongst the troops' and recording that he had no more than 17,000 men instead of the 28,000-30,000 that he had hoped to command. He was trying to replace the lost men by raising new levies in Germany. Moreover, he advised Philip that the English and their Dutch allies were now properly prepared to confront the Armada. He lamented Santa Cruz's death and looked forward to working with Medina Sidonia, but he did so warily – 'I will cooperate with him in all openness and sincerity…and I hope that he, on his side, will act in the same way'. That carried the implication that Parma feared that his relationship with Medina Sidonia might prove to be difficult. Parma informed Philip, moreover, that he was fearful of mutinies among his men because he was so short of funds with which to pay them. He urgently needed money, therefore, to levy more troops and also to leave the Low Countries properly defended while he was across the Channel. He asked Philip to forgive his boldness 'and to accept all I say as prompted only by my zeal and affection for your service'.[20] He looked to the negotiations with the English not as a cover for his preparations but in the hope that they would prove to be successful and thereby release him from the campaign. In short, Parma feared that the Enterprise of England would greatly damage his own reputation and he wanted to be free of it.

There was, indeed, much controversy and debate at court in England about the defensive strategy to be employed. Drake was grandly promising to disable the Armada in Lisbon, or at the very least to inflict so much damage on it as to

Statue of Don Álvaro de Bazán, Marquis of Santa Cruz, Madrid, (1526-88).

Statue of Sir Francis Drake (1543-96), Plymouth Hoe.

Don Pedro de Valdés.

Statue of Lope de Vega (1562-1635), Madrid.

prevent it from sailing. But the privateer had many opponents at court, and some of them hinted that he was really intent on privateering for his own advantage rather than carrying out a carefully considered strategic plan designed to ensure the security of the realm. There were those, too, who argued that Drake should not be allowed to take any of the Queen's ships away from home waters as the risks would be too great – an argument which events in 1596-7 were to support. And still there remained some who hoped that war could be avoided. Chief among these were Elizabeth herself, who clung to the hope that the peace commissioners might reach an agreement with Parma. And so too did many of the Queen's Catholic subjects, who hoped even now to be released from the pressures that the arrival of the Armada would place upon them to choose between their queen and their faith. But preparations went energetically ahead for war and as men drilled and ships were made ready, the government's propaganda machine was whipping up stories that Philip had vowed that no English person aged between seven and seventy would be left alive by the beginning of 1589. In the welter of preparations, the details of the English fleet became as well-known as those of the Spanish.[21]

On 1 April, Philip dispatched Medina Sidonia's orders. He recognized that the delay since he had issued instructions to Parma in September 1587 had given the enemy time to organize. The duke was ordered to 'sail with the...Armada, and go straight to the English Channel, where you will ascend as far as Cape Margate, where you will join the duke of Parma...and hold the passage for his crossing'. Philip insisted that there should be close communication between Medina Sidonia and Parma and that the admiral should not allow himself to be diverted by Drake from proceeding to his objective. Nevertheless, Philip gave the duke permission to engage Elizabeth's fleet if the opportunity presented itself, although he thought it likely that the English would fight at long range. He warned Medina Sidonia against over-eagerness; above all, the Armada must retain its discipline and not be drawn into unnecessary skirmishes. Philip sternly warned Medina Sidonia not to allow the Armada to follow up a victory against the English by losing its discipline in pursuit of the remnants of the Royal Navy. He laid down strict orders about the distribution of prizes and booty. If he did not have to fight the English, Medina Sidonia was to hand over to Parma 6,000 Spanish troops. He should then station the Armada at the entrance to the Thames to support the invasion, while a number of ships should be put on patrol to prevent reinforcement reaching the English from the continent. In this he stressed that Medina Sidonia's 'sole function' was to fight at sea. Philip emphasized the need to cooperate with Parma, for victory would bring honour enough for both of them. In reminding Medina Sidonia of this, Philip was mindful of the need to insist that his commanders did not pursue individual glory: the masterplan was to be followed in every detail. After victory was assured, Medina Sidonia could return to Spain, 'settling affairs in Ireland on the way' if Parma gave permission for him to do so. Philip allowed Medina Sidonia to alter the details of the plan as circumstances arose but strictly enjoined him that he was not to change the plans themselves 'in any way'.[22] A distinguished naval historian has observed that 'Philip's inflexible orders to make no independent landing but to embark Parma's troops condemned the...Armada to certain failure'.[23]

Secret orders accompanied these formal instructions. Medina Sidonia carried a sealed envelope that was to be given to Parma only after he had landed in England or had shown 'uncertainty' about being able to do so. Philip reminded Medina Sidonia that when he arrived off Cape Margate he would learn where Parma required him to disembark troops under the command of Don Alonso de Leiva, one of Parma's lieutenants. Philip hardly dared bring himself to contemplate failure, but he instructed Medina Sidonia that:

'if, for our sins,...the Duke should be unable to cross to England, or you unable to form a junction with him, you will, after communication with him, consider whether you cannot seize the Isle of Wight, which is apparently not so strong as to be able to resist, and may be defended if we gain it. This will provide for you a safe port for shelter, and will enable you to carry out such operations as may be rendered possible by the importance of the position. It will therefore be advisable for you to fortify yourself strongly there.'[24]

In his sealed instructions for Parma, Philip ordered his nephew that if the Armada did fail to join with and transport his troops he was to negotiate the best possible terms with Elizabeth. He was to secure 'the free use and exercise of our holy Catholic faith' for all Catholics and permission for those who had taken refuge abroad to return home. The English were to surrender to Spain the fortresses they held in the Low Countries and they should recompense Philip for the 'exceedingly great sum' that their activities and involvement had caused him to spend.

Philip also set out a remarkable statement about the advantages that followed from the freedom of religious practice and urged that Parma impress upon Elizabeth that 'there will be no sacrifice of dignity' in allowing English Catholics to practice their religion freely. After all, such freedom was allowed in France! If the English replied that Philip himself did not allow freedom of religion in the Low Countries, Parma was to insist that the English would enjoy the benefits of religious toleration because 'people from all Christendom would flock thither in the assurance of safety, whilst the commerce of Englishmen in other countries would be carried on without the present vexations'.[25]

The general who was to ensure victory continued to complain unremittingly about the preparations. Parma insisted to Philip that if the Armada had come months before, the Enterprise of England would have been 'so easy and safe'[26] but now he was having to support 59,915 men while merely waiting for the

Armada to leave port.[27] But similar logistical problems were also affecting Elizabeth's navy. The Spanish received detailed accounts of the size and capacity of the English fleet[28] and of the difficulties of raising men and feeding them. Indeed, even Drake himself was finding that his men were deserting as he failed to depart for his attack on the Armada. From Paris, Mendoza reported that fifty-two English ships were stationed at Queenborough. But Philip was encouraged by reports that Elizabeth's ships were not in good condition and did not have enough gunpowder.[29]

Meanwhile Medina Sidonia was working zealously to prepare the fleet to sail. On 21 April he issued instructions for the management of the provisions (which were already rotting away rapidly). Each man was to receive one-and-a-half pounds of biscuit daily or two pounds of fresh bread. The duke stipulated the size of the daily rations of wine, bacon and rice; he even laid down precise instructions concerning the order in which the casks were to be opened. Lists of men were to be drawn up and verified. Ship notaries were to check everything.[30] Medina Sidonia was a superb organizer and he drew up a precise survey of the great fleet as it stood ready to depart from Lisbon. The muster of 9 May showed that the fleet consisted of 130 ships, sixty-five of them men-of-war. It had twenty-five hulks, nineteen dispatch boats or pataches, thirteen Biscay smacks ('*zabras*') and four galleasses. These latter warships could be propelled by oarsmen when there was not enough wind to fill their sails; in calm seas they could be rowed quickly over short distances. Medina Sidonia had only four galleys, one-tenth of the number that Santa Cruz had planned for in 1583. For the record, the total tonnage of the fleet was 57,868 *toneladas* – a figure which did not include the ten caravels and ten armed *faluas*. The fleet carried 30,693 men, of whom 8,052 were sailors (2,088 of them on the galleasses and galleys). There were 16,973 Spanish soldiers and 2,000 Portuguese. There were 124 gentlemen adventurers, some of them Irish and perhaps even a few English. Not all those embarked upon the Armada were fighting men; gentlemen had to have their own servants and Medina Sidonia set the benchmark by taking a household consisting of twenty-two gentlemen and fifty personal servants. The volunteers took 465 servants with them. The spiritual needs of the fleet were met by 180 religious men, both secular and ordinary. Eighty-five hospital staff were carried to deal with illness and battle injuries – a remarkably small number, less than one per ship. The provisions, which were itemized in impressive detail, were to be dealt with by an Inspector-general and his staff of sixteen. Law and order was in the hands of eighteen law officers; a company of notaries were to itemize every detail of expenditure on armaments and provisions. The provisions were, in theory at least, sufficient for six months [Appendix I].[31]

On the same day as the muster – 9 May 1588 – the Armada moved from Lisbon to Belem and edged out to sea. Sailing into and out of harbour was traditionally the most difficult and dangerous task for large ships even in good weather but strong winds whipped up and the fleet had to return to the

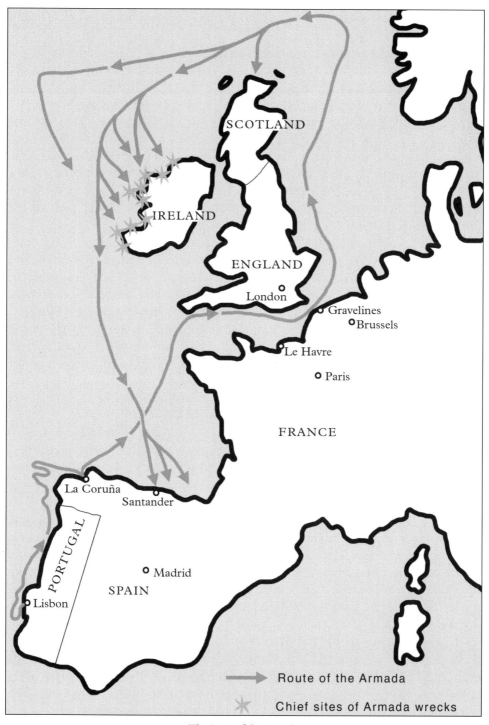

SCOTLAND

IRELAND

ENGLAND

o London

o Gravelines
o Brussels

Le Havre

o Paris

FRANCE

La Coruña
Santander

PORTUGAL

o Madrid

SPAIN

o Lisbon

⟶ Route of the Armada

✳ Chief sites of Armada wrecks

The Route of the Armada.

harbour. Medina Sidonia wrote to Philip that God 'has not seen fit to send weather for the sailing of the Armada. It is as boisterous and as bad as if it were December'.[32] It was not an auspicious beginning.

Elizabeth herself could not afford to keep large armed forces on alert but she knew that she had the organization in place to ensure that the mobilization could be rapidly brought about when the time came. Throughout 1587 Elizabeth only kept small patrols at sea and not until November 1587 did she order a partial mobilization. Drake was sent down to Plymouth to join with Howard to guard the Western Approaches while Sir Henry Palmer lay in the Narrow Seas with another squadron to prevent Parma from making a sudden sortie. Early in January 1588, the English had fewer than thirty ships ready for action, and these were garrisoned with just 4,000 men. Not surprisingly, Elizabeth hoped that war could be avoided.[33]

Her commander, however, was eager for action. Howard was intensely proud of his ships – 'I do thank God that they be in the estate they be in; and there is never a one of them that knows what a leak means' he wrote to Burghley at the beginning of March.[34] A week later he was even more enthusiastic: 'I protest before God, and as my soul shall answer for it, that I think there were never in any place in the world worthier ships than these are, for so many. And as few as we are, if the King of Spain's forces be not hundreds, we will make good sport with them'.[35] Drake shared Howard's eagerness for the fray but advised the government that the Armada was a formidable force – 'there was never any force so strong as there is now ready or making ready against your Majesty and true religion'.[36]

On 31 May, Howard sailed for Plymouth, leaving Lord Henry Seymour with a squadron in the Downs. On 10 and 29 June and again on 3 July Drake's fleet left Plymouth to attack the Armada but each time it was blown back by storms. By 22 July it was at anchor in Plymouth.[37] The Armada would be fought in the Channel.

Medina Sidonia issued his general orders to his fleet at some unknown time in May. His first concern was to stress that this was Philip's personal crusade for God, and to implement the injunctions for the proper conduct and behaviour mentioned above. He then turned to more secular matters. Strenuous efforts were to be made to ensure that there was no friction between the soldiers and the sailors. The fleet was to sail in close order and any captain not following orders was to be executed.[38]

A final muster of the Armada was held in Lisbon on 28 May. It showed that the fleet now consisted of 141 ships totalling 60,151 *toneladas* and carried 26,961 men – 7,666 seamen and 19,295 soldiers. Even now, more soldiers were embarked, and the fleet may have carried as many as 33,000-35,000 men when it finally sailed. The 'Spanish Armada' carried men of many nations; the largest number of soldiers (8,000) were Germans while there were around 7,000 Walloons, 6,000 Spaniards, 3,000 Italians, 1,000 Irishmen and 1,000 Burgundians.[39]

Medina Sidonia professed himself confident of success. He had been advised that he would be able to 'break up the enemy's sea force' in the Channel if the English dared to give him battle, and once this was done 'the rest will be safe and easy.' Indeed, his biggest concern was that the English might thwart his strategy by refusing to fight him: 'Trusting to the mercy of God that if the enemy will face us he will meet the fate he always has done when he has encountered your Majesty's forces', he looked forward to an easy land campaign once the fleet had defeated the Royal Navy. He led the fleet out of Lisbon harbour on 28 May 1588.[40] It consisted of six fighting squadrons totalling sixty-three men of war – the two royal squadrons of Castile and Portugal, a further two from Guipúzcoa and one each from Andalusia and the Levant. Four large galleasses from Naples and four galleys carried soldiers on board. Even small caravels had some soldiers on board. Twenty-three hulks were loaded with supplies. The fleet presented a brilliant, awesome, spectacle but the last major embarkation of men had taken place as long ago as 13 April and the last provisions had been brought on board on 9 May. Medina Sidonia would have to be as mindful of the condition of his victuals as he would of the English fleet.

As the fleet edged out into the Ocean Sea the weather changed and Medina Sidonia was anxious that, far from progressing regally northwards up the Iberian coast, his fleet would be driven south by the winds. He had to tack out to sea and wait for better weather. Not until 9 June did the fleet begin to move to the north. But still, the duke was confident; he wrote to Parma that his men were in good heart 'ready for the fight if the enemy will face us'. But beneath his confidence was a worry that was clearly gnawing at him, for he knew that the Channel coast was not 'capable of sheltering so great a fleet as this'. Tacking into the wind and praying for success, Medina Sidonia set sail up the Iberian coast.[41]

Confronting bad weather and progressing at the speed of his slowest vessel, it took Medina Sidnona two weeks to sail the length of the coast and he decided to put in to La Coruña to refresh the water supplies. On 19 June the *San Martin* led the way into port but only fifty ships had berthed when at midnight a violent storm arose – 'the people of the country say that so violent a sea and wind, accompanied by fog and tempest, have never been seen'. Medina Sidonia feared that he had lost his fleet even before approaching the enemy: 'I find myself here with the best of the Armada out at sea'. While he waited anxiously for news of his ships, he sent out for provisions to be brought to him, but Galicia was a poor region and could provide little. He kept iron discipline to prevent desertions. However, the paucity of the provisions and the unhygienic conditions on board were causing great damage: 'many men are falling sick, aided by the short commons and bad food, and I am afraid that this trouble may spread and become past remedy'.[42] In England, Howard was excited to hear that the Armada was scattered along the Spanish coast – 'dispersed into sundry ports of Spain, distressed, spoiled, in necessity of victuals and [with] great mortality grown amongst their people'.[43] It seemed that perhaps a higher force was at work. Howard determined to attack the Armada in Spain if possible.

The setback at La Coruña caused a severe if short bout of pessimism in Medina Sidonia. On 24 June he wrote to Philip effectively urging him to abandon the expedition. 'I have hitherto delayed saying to your Majesty what I am now about to say', he began, but he was 'impelled by my conscientious duty to your Majesty' to make representations to him about continuing the Enterprise. He confessed that when he had accepted command of the expedition he already knew that it was not strong enough – 'I recognized that we were attacking a kingdom so powerful, and so warmly aided by its neighbours that we should need a much larger force than your Majesty had collected at Lisbon'. The fleet that he now had at La Coruña was 'much inferior in strength to the enemy according to the opinion of all those who are competent to judge'. Many of the most important ships were still missing. The men in La Coruña were falling sick and the provisions were 'so scanty that there cannot be more than sufficient to last two months'. The Armada was the very strength of Philip's monarchy and if it was lost Medina Sidonia could see no means of replacing it. The defences of the monarchy would be stripped bare from Flanders to the Caribbean. He was in despair: 'I am bound to confess that I see very few, or hardly any, of those on the Armada with any knowledge of or ability to perform the duties entrusted to them. I have tested and watched this point very carefully, and your Majesty may believe me when I assure you that we are very weak'. He also stressed that Parma had a comparatively small force and that the two forces combined 'would still be weak, but if we do not join we shall be feeble indeed'. Medina Sidonia recalled the great force that had been required to conquer Portugal and asked Philip: 'Well, sire, how do you think we can attack so great a country as England with such a force as ours is now?' He suggested that Philip should negotiate the best terms that he could with Elizabeth – 'making some honourable terms with the enemy'.[44]

Three days after writing to Philip, Medina Sidonia summoned a council of war on the *San Martín*. Twenty-eight ships were still missing, and with them 6,000 men. He was joined by his squadron commanders – Martínez de Recalde, Flores de Valdés, Pedro de Valdés, Oquendo, Bertendona, López de Medina, Hurtado de Mendoza, Moncada and Medrano – and by Francisco de Bobadilla and Jorge de Manrique. Medina Sidonia opened the discussion by asking, somewhat ingenuously perhaps, whether the ships that were in La Coruña should remain there or go out and seek the missing vessels. The council was unanimous in urging him to remain in the harbour and wait for the missing ships to turn up. The duke then asked for advice as to whether the Armada should resume its campaign. He required each man to state his view for the record. The subsequent discussion is of value because it provides an expert analysis of the strategic and logistic circumstances of the Armada.

The majority view was expressed by Don Jorge Manrique and Francisco de Bobadilla. Manrique began with the bare figures. One-third of the fleet was missing, including some of the best ships and its finest soldiers. He stressed how catastrophic the consequences would be 'for Christendom and the preservation of his Majesty's monarchy' if the Armada were defeated. The *proveedor general* did not want to proceed with the fleet in its present condition. Bobadilla made a similar point. He insisted that if the Armada was at full strength 'its task was safe and easy' but if not 'the risk would be great, especially in face of the forces the enemy now had'. In the event of the Armada being defeated, Portugal and Flanders would be 'in dire peril'. Don Francisco therefore stated with all the conviction of his formidable personality that the Armada should remain in La Coruña until it was reassembled as the powerful fleet that had left Lisbon.

Not many men dared to argue with Bobadilla but Pedro de Valdés now proceeded to do so. Indeed, he spoke contemptuously of the argument that the Armada should not proceed on its mission. It was in his view obvious that the enemy forces would be divided into two or three units and it was certainly evident that the Armada would soon reassemble in full strength; to his mind, the storm had not been that violent. He admitted that the provisions on his own squadron were generally in dire condition – 'there was more than enough wine for three months, but the bacon, cheese, fish, sardines and vegetables were all rotten and of very little use' – and suggested that fresh meat should be supplied to the men while they were in La Coruña. He omitted to state how such provisions were to be supplied from one of the poorest regions of Spain. His colleagues seized the opportunity to reiterate the many complaints that the men on board were making about the food – 'with the exception of the bread (and that is very bad) the wine, rice and some of the pulse, the victuals were of no use whatever, for the men would not eat them'.

Manrique accepted that the complaints were justified: 'with the exception of the bread, the wine and the vegetables, everything was spoilt and rotten, as it had been on board so long.' But still, he considered that there was food enough for a further eighty days, except – he waspishly added – on Pedro de Valdés's squadron, where there might be enough for ninety. The commanders drew a blunt conclusion from what Manrique had said: 'it was unanimously agreed that the stores were insufficient for so large a force'. Each man signed the report, and it was sent to Philip on 28 June. A few days later, Pedro de Valdés himself wrote to the king, noting that since his views had differed so much from those of his colleagues, Medina Sidonia was 'looking upon him with an unfriendly eye, and had used expressions towards him which had greatly grieved him'.[45]

Philip paid no heed to the advice from La Coruña, dismissing out of hand Medina Sidonia's misgivings in a letter of 1 July. He insisted: 'I have dedicated this service to God, and have taken you as an instrument to assist me in it'. Clearly, being an instrument of God allowed for no faintheartedness. There was to be no retreat from the plan. But Philip himself was again crumbling under stress.[46] Four days later, he ordered that the Armada was to be reassembled and re-fitted, and that it was to sail within days, probably by 10-12 July. Medina Sidonia was to prepare to leave within an hour of receiving the order to do so.[47]

It was a mark of the pressure that Medina Sidonia was feeling that his mood swung once again, and by 6 July he was writing optimistically to the king. Most of the missing ships were now accounted for in ports near to La Coruña and the duke was even prepared to consider that it was a blessing that the storm had struck the fleet off the Spanish coast rather than at the entrance to the Channel, where it could have found no safe refuge in which it could gather itself. However, he informed Philip that the first signs of fever had appeared among his men.[48]

On 21-22 July Medina Sidonia once again led his fleet to sea. He took 127 ships out of La Coruña – twenty galleons and four galleasses, forty-four armed merchantmen, thirty-eight auxiliaries and twenty-one supply ships. Certainly, the English knew that they were expecting a mighty force; Hawkins himself would write of 'the greatest and strongest combination, to my understanding, that was ever gathered in Christendom'.[49]

6 Battle: The Channel and the Northern Seas, 23 July – 3 September

The summer of 1588 presented the optimum conditions for the English and probably the worst conditions for the Spanish. True, it could be objected that a realistic assessment of the tasks and risks involved in such an enterprise would have made it inevitable that around thirty months of preparations would be required. However, it is clear that the plans and proposals made to Philip II in the years 1585-6 had been based upon the supposition that the Armada would enjoy the advantage of surprise. Elizabeth received a flood of spy reports over 1586, some of them detailing plans made at the highest level of Philip's government – two copies of Santa Cruz's plan for the invasion fell into Elizabeth's hands. Spanish commanders had planned to have completed the naval operations by June, and certainly by July, in order to give time to Parma to march on London before the campaigning season ended. The mere fact that the Armada would reach the coast of England in the last days of July and would fight Lord Howard's fleet in the first weeks of August can be seen as a serious disadvantage for Philip II's fleet.

The details of the Armada campaign can be summarized as follows. The fleet moved into the Channel in late July; as it did so it was shadowed by the English navy, which divided into squadrons and was able to inflict relatively modest damage upon the Spanish fleet at relatively high risk to itself: Drake and Howard were fortunate to escape from a high-risk attack upon a stricken Spanish vessel. The defensive crescent formation adopted by Medina Sidonia was highly effective; as long as it maintained this disciplined shape it was practically impossible for the English to inflict major damage on it. True, the duke of Medina Sidonia could not maintain this formation indefinitely; he had to try to establish a base – an attempt to disembark at the Isle of Wight was successfully repelled by the English, who used the tides to their advantage – and then collect Parma. This was the decisive point of the campaign, the pivot around which history would turn: could the Spanish coordinate the arrival of the Armada with the embarkation of the Army of Flanders? As we know, it could not. While anchored off Calais, as Medina Sidonia frantically attempted to sort out with Parma the details of the linking operation, the Armada was scattered by English fireships. An intense battle then took place; neither side could claim victory, although the accounts always suggest that the Spanish

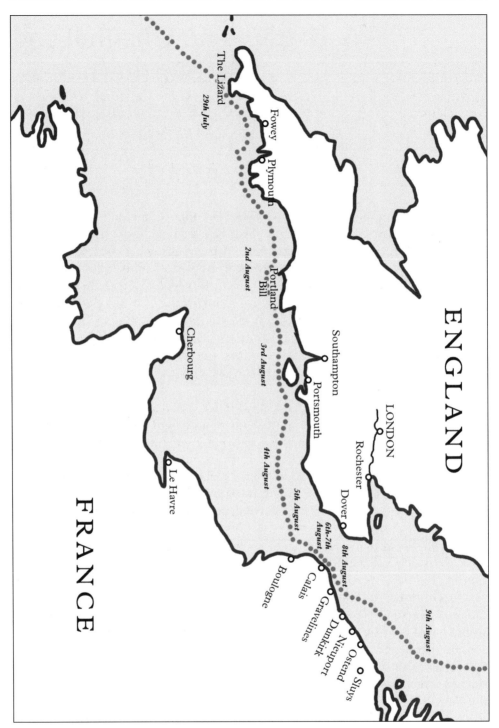

The Armada in the Channel.

fleet sustained heavier damage than did the English. Nevertheless, the Armada, if now not quite deserving the title 'invincible', could still at least be described as 'undefeated.' But now it was at the mercy of Providence, or tides and winds. God's design was now in His hands. Forced by winds to head north around Scotland and Ireland, Philip's fleet was mercilessly pounded by the elements, which inflicted more damage than had Elizabeth's dreadnoughts. The remnants of the Armada arrived back in Spain in early September – a point of the year better described as late summer than early autumn, and well before the traditional campaigning season in the Mediterranean had drawn to a close. The battle of Lepanto, for example, was fought on 7 October.

The voyage across Biscay went relatively smoothly. On 25 July Medina Sidonia sent Don Rodrigo Tello to Dunkirk to inform Parma that he had departed and to find out what the state of preparedness of his army was and where the junction with the Armada was to take place. But once again the weather intervened to blow the fleet off course; on 27 July a storm separated a number of ships and the three remaining galleys from the fleet. The Armada sustained a number of losses; the Santa Ana, flagship of Martínez de Recalde, ran ahead of the fleet and was forced to take refuge in Le Havre, where she stayed for the remainder of the campaign, and the remaining three galleys lay up in port in the Bay of Biscay and also took no further part in the campaign.[1]

The Spanish fleet formed a shape roughly like a crescent for its voyage up the Channel. Bertendona's Levant Squadron and the galleasses commanded by Hugo de Moncada led the way, with the *San Martín* and a squadron of galleons comprising the main body of the fleet. The two wings of the crescent were taken by the Andalusian Squadron under Pedro de Valdés, and the Guipuzcoans under Miguel de Oquendo. The Biscayan Squadron under Martínez de Recalde made up the rearguard. The crescent was maintained by high seamanship but it presented the danger that the ships could collide with each other and it made it difficult for them to use all their guns against the English.

At around four o'clock on the afternoon of 29 July, the coast of England was sighted from the Armada when The Lizard came into view. But the fleet was itself seen for the first time by the English; Captain Thomas Fleming raced the *Golden Hind* to Plymouth to be the first with the news.[2] Legend has it that Drake heard the news when he was playing bowls but refused to stop the game, claiming that he had time enough to finish the game and then deal with the Spaniards. This story is probably not true, for Drake would have known better than anyone how complex would be the operation that was now required to get the fleet out of Plymouth Harbour before the Spanish could catch it there. If the game of bowls did exist, in all probability it was cut short when Captain Fleming brought his momentous news.

At daybreak on 30 July the Armada glimpsed its first sight of enemy ships. The weather was, again, very poor – 'thick and rainy' – and the English vessels

The Armada off the Lizard, 29 July 1588.

The Armada off Fowey, 30 July 1588.

could not be counted. Ensign Juan Gil was sent in a rowing boat to find news; he returned with four unhappy Englishmen from Falmouth, who reported that the English fleet, under the Lord Admiral and Drake, had sailed from Plymouth late in the previous evening. This had been no easy feat. Our only account records that 'with that wind were very hard to be gotten out of harbour' but it was done 'with such diligence and good will, that many of

The first engagement, 31 July 1588.

them got abroad as though it had been with a fair wind'.[3] However it was done it was a brilliant feat of seamanship. The English fleet sailed out of its home base almost two months to the day after the Spanish left Lisbon.

The Armada sighted eighty ships to windward of it in Plymouth Roads and a further dozen or so to leeward. The first cannonade of the campaign was fired by the English. Medina Sidonia raised the royal standard and ordered the Armada to battle stations. The English launched their attack, limited as it was, at about 9.00am, in line-ahead formation. Successive ships moved into action to fire at the enemy before retreating to reload. They could not get near the troop carriers and concentrated on the warships of the Spanish left wing, which was commanded by Alonso de Leiva. The Spanish could not respond effectively, for they were unable to reload their heavy guns quickly enough.

The English then turned on the Spanish rearguard commanded by Juan Martínez de Recalde, although again this led to no more than light skirmishing. Drake moved in with Frobisher and Hawkins. The *Revenge*, *Victory*, and the *Triumph* drew to within 300yds of its Spanish prey. Martínez de Recalde, commanding the *San Juan de Portugal*, decided to fight even though he was being left behind. It may be that he was trying to provoke the English into coming to close quarters so that he could grapple and board them. At all events, he distinguished himself for the first of many times in the campaign. His vessel took a withering storm of fire in which his rigging was crippled and his masts damaged. He was supported by the other vessels of the Biscayan contingent, including the *Gran Grin*. Medina Sidonia ordered the fleet to wait for Martínez de Recalde to rejoin it. The English moved away at about 1.00pm, determined not to be drawn into fighting at close quarters.

The capture of the San Salvador, 2 August 1588.

Medina Sidonia tried to attack them, but to no avail; the English were too nimble.

The Armada had demonstrated its discipline, but at about five o'clock in the afternoon it also had its first experience of the dangers that were involved in sailing in such close formation, when Pedro de Valdés's flagship, the *Nuestra Señora del Rosario* crashed into the *Catalina* and damaged its bowsprit and foresail. Almost immediately, Miguel de Oquendo's vice-flagship, the *San Salvador* – the ship carrying the Paymaster General of the Armada and a large part of the treasure of the fleet – was rocked by an explosion which destroyed two decks and the poop castle and caused a serious fire. About half of the 500 men on board were wounded or killed. Medina Sidonia dispatched four *pataches* to assist; they brought some of the survivors off but there was little they could do for the seriously wounded. The admiral brought his own flagship, the *San Martin*, to help. Medina Sidonia had shown that he would lead by example. It was soon evident that the *San Salvador* was a liability and had to be abandoned and sunk. But her captain (Pedro de Priego) had been badly wounded and the men were in such a hurry to leave the ship that no one remained to sink her. John Hawkins and Lord Thomas Howard briefly boarded the hulk to assess the damage but 'the stink in the ship was so unsavoury and the sight within board so ugly' that they quickly left.[4] She was towed into Weymouth.

The *Nuestra Señora del Rosario* was becoming a heavy liability, especially when her foremast collapsed. At first she was towed, but she inevitably lagged behind the fleet and her continued presence threatened to endanger the ships towing her. Don Pedro Valdés and his ship had to be abandoned. Medina Sidonia made one last attempt to save the vessel, sending four *pataches* to tow her or recover her complement of men. However, the heavy seas and the proximity of the enemy fleet meant that neither aim could be achieved. Medina Sidonia decided that Valdés had to be abandoned.

Howard called a council to discuss tactics. He gave Drake the honour of leading the fleet; the remainder of the fleet were to follow lantern. It was now the evening on 31 July. However, in perhaps the most remarkable act of self-indulgence in his entire career, Drake extinguished his lanterns and made off into the night. This act endangered not only the ships under his command, but all those who were taking their lead from his lantern. Howard was alarmed to find at daybreak that the *Ark Royal* – accompanied by the *Bear* and the *Mary Rose* – was within firing range of the wings of the Spanish crescent; he had mistaken the Armada's light for Drake's. Howard was detached from his own fleet. Medina Sidonia should have launched an assault, perhaps using the galleasses, which could have made good speed over a short distance, but he failed to do so and the three English ships escaped.

Having led Howard into danger, Drake at least succeeded in capturing his prey, the *Nuestra Señora del Rosario*. Don Pedro de Valdés appears to have been unnerved when Drake identified himself, and he offered no resistance when the celebrated privateer invited him to surrender; he knew full well what would happen if he did not. It was the first loss of the campaign in battle. Along with Valdés, Captain Vicente Álvarez, the owner of the ship, 128 sailors and about 150 soldiers were captured. Some 50,000 ducats belonging to the King were also taken.[5]

Off Portland Bill on 31 July, Martin Frobisher tried to trap the galleasses by drawing them on to the shoals. But the wind changed and the Spanish were able to escape. Despite these minor difficulties, the Armada moved with unflinching discipline up the Channel. It adopted the crescent formation. However, it moved very slowly, at the pace of its slowest ships. The need to communicate with Parma was becoming more urgent by the day, for he would need at least six days to prepare his forces. The problem was that he did not even know that the Armada was approaching; in contrast, Medina Sidonia believed that Parma was ready and waiting for him.

Later that afternoon, Medina Sidonia ordered Alonso de Leiva to join the vanguard with the rearguard to form one body; he was to take the three galleasses and the galleons *San Mateo*, *San Luís*, *Florencia* and *Santiago* and form a squadron of forty-three of the best ships of the fleet. Their purpose was to protect the Armada in the Channel while it made the junction with Parma. Medina Sidonia led the vanguard, comprised of the other ships, essentially the bulkier ships which would be less adept at fighting. He then sent the intrepid Juan Gil in a *patache* to inform Parma of his position.[6] On 2 August the commanders of the Armada awoke off Portland Bill to find the English still trying to gain the wind. Medina Sidonia did likewise. Medina Sidonia in the *San Martín* engaged the enemy fleet for an hour and a half. The details of this encounter support the contention that the English were able to discharge their artillery more quickly than their adversaries could: the *San Martín* fired over

The capture of the Nuestra Señora del Rosario.

The surrender of Don Pedro de Valdés to Francis Drake, Seymour Lucas..

eighty shots from one side only, causing great damage. But the English shot over 500 cannon balls at the *San Martín*, striking both hull and rigging, and carrying away the flagstaff. The skirmish lasted from dawn until 10.00am. But then the wind shifted to the north, which enabled the English to gain the wind and they continued firing for another five hours. Bertendona, leading a

The Armada re-engaged, between Portland Bill and the Isle of Wight, 2-3 August 1588.

number of the best fighting ships including the *San Marcos, San Luís, San Mateo, La Rata, San Felipe, San Juan de Sicilia, Santiago, San Juan, Valencera*, counter-attacked the English flagship and managed to draw close to it, but not, however, near enough to board. During this skirmish Medina Sidonia ordered the galleasses into action. But, again, the Spanish were not able to catch the English, who skipped impudently out of range. Later that day the English took advantage of wind and tide to attack Martínez de Recalde's ship. Alonso de Leiva came to his assistance.[7]

Despite the fact that the English had had the better of the skirmishes, there was cause for concern among their commanders. The Armada was moving irresistibly ahead. Howard called a conference of his captains It was decided to organize the English fleet into four squadrons, to be commanded by Howard, Drake, Hawkins and Frobisher.[8] On 3 August there was heavy fighting off the Isle of Wight. The English had to ensure that the Spanish did not attempt a landing. The strategic value of the island in the Solent was considerable in light of the need to communicate with the governor-general of the Netherlands; Medina Sidonia and Parma could coordinate the rendezvous from the Isle of Wight or from an anchorage in the Solent. If the Spanish did not settle in the Solent, then the problem of corresponding with Parma was increased several-fold. It would be difficult to coordinate the arrival and preparedness of the fleet; it would also be necessary for the fleet to anchor off the coast of the Low Countries, and this was made dangerous by the conjunction of tide, sand-dunes and Dutch and English fleets.

Was it Drake who attacked now and drove them away from the eastern Solent, forcing them to move towards Calais? The loss of many English

The battle off the Isle of Wight, 4 August 1588.

records makes it difficult to know for certain. At all events, it was a very important engagement. However, it moved past the Solent, unable to contemplate turning round to land men on the Isle of Wight with the English close at hand. Medina Sidonia now knew that he had to follow the king's plan and sail for the Straits and on for Margate.

On 4 August the hulks, *Santa Ana* and *Doncella*, and a Portuguese galleon fell behind. As the English ships, *Ark Royal* and the *Golden Lion*, moved in to attack them, Medina Sidonia again ordered Alonso de Leiva to take his galleasses into action, and they succeeded in towing the *La Rata Coronada* to safety. The two squadrons were engaged in an intense artillery confrontation. The three galleasses sustained some damage but they were able to tow the *San Luis* and the *Santa Ana* away from their assailants.

Although Elizabeth could be very pleased with the performance of a number of her captains – Howard knighted Hawkins and Frobisher in the middle of the campaign – the details of the skirmishes suggests that the Armada had not hitherto sustained serious damage. The decisive moment of the summer was about to begin. Everything depended upon the Spanish being able to coordinate the collection of Parma's army.

On 5 August, the wind fell calm before daybreak and the Armada remained motionless all day. Medina Sidonia dispatched another *patache* to Parma under Domingo Ochoa.[9] Parma was asked to send 40 flyboats out to join Medina Sidonia in order to help the fleet draw closer to the English. Ochoa was to insist that Parma be ready to come out to join the Armada when it appeared in sight of Dunkirk.

On Saturday 6 August the coast of France came into view. The Armada was off Boulogne. Medina Sidonia was faced with a difficult situation in that there

The Armada pursued towards Calais, 4-6 August 1588.

was no possibility of taking harbour in Calais and Parma could not move his troops out to meet him because a fleet of thirty or so small Dutch ships under Justin of Nassau was preventing him from sallying from harbour. The Armada moved to Calais Roads, where it arrived at four in the afternoon. The commanders gave differing advice as to whether the fleet should anchor there; the majority opinion was that the fleet should move on. However, the pilots informed Medina Sidonia that if he proceeded further the currents might well force him out into the North Sea, and so in the late afternoon the fateful order was sent to drop anchor. He was 35km from Dunkirk.

That afternoon Lord Henry Seymour arrived with a further thirty-six or so ships, including five large galleons, to reinforce the English fleet. They included the two most modern English ships, the *Rainbow* and the *Vanguard*. The entire English fleet, now 160 sail strong, took up position a league or so away from the Armada; in desperation Medina Sidonia sent Secretary Arceo and Don Jorge Manrique to Parma to inform him that it was impossible for the Armada to remain where it was without running great risk. Arceo returned with news that evening that Parma had not yet arrived at Dunkirk and that the supplies had not been taken on board the boats. It would take a fortnight for the embarkation at Dunkirk to be completed.[10] The invasion of England was now practically of the question.

Who was to blame? Many placed the failure of the fleet upon the head of Parma. Recent research has, however, revealed the extent of the preparations made by the governor-general of the Netherlands in the years 1586-8. Instead, the failure to coordinate the collection of the Army of Flanders is now blamed on a flaw in the plan itself; it might have been much better to embark Parma's men – or certainly a portion of them – in Lisbon or La Coruña as Santa Cruz

The attack of the fireships off Calais, 7 August 1588.

had proposed. It might even have been better to run the gauntlet of the Dutch flyboats, the English navy and the seas in a fleet of flat-boats sailing from Dunkirk than to undertake the plan upon which Philip had finally settled.[11] These thoughts can have brought little consolation to Medina Sidonia as he faced the fact that he had been hemmed into port and was supremely vulnerable.

At sunset the English fleet was joined by nine ships, and a squadron of more than a score of ships moved closer towards them. With dread, the Spaniards realized that the English were about to launch fireboats. Medina Sidonia ordered a Captain Serrano to take a pinnace and do what he could to divert any fireships away from the fleet and towards the shore and he had rowing boats prepared to serve the same purpose. The fleet stood on alert. At midnight, two fires could be made out in the distance, and then more appeared until, in all, eight were visible. They had their sails set and were drifting with the current directly towards the *San Martín*. As they came closer, the Spanish could see that they ranged in size from about 90-200 tons. They were burning furiously and coming straight at the fleet. Huddled together in close formation, the Armada could not move, and terror spread as the dread apparition approached. Many of the soldiers on board were veterans of Antwerp in 1585 and all knew of the dreadful chaos that Gambelli's 'Hellburners' had caused. In fact, it was bluff; the ships were not packed with explosives. The Spanish, however, dared not wait for them to arrive and broke ranks. Medina Sidonia ordered the fleet to disperse and then to regroup after the fireships had either been towed away or drifted past them. He cut the *San Martín* free and moved 8km out to sea before dropping anchor. The other ships followed suit. In fact the English ships were not infernal machines packed with explosive, but they had done as much damage as if they had been. The Spanish formation had broken and the Armada was dispersed into small groups of ships. As dawn broke the *San Martín* stood alone with only four great Portuguese galleons – the *San Juan*; the *San Marcos*; the *San Felipe* and *San Mateo*. The only other ship that Medina Sidonia could see was the galleass *San Lorenzo*, which was drifting rudderless towards the shore. (It later transpired that she had run into the *San Juan de Sicilia* and her rudder had been broken.) The rest of the Armada had drifted off in the strong current in the direction of Dunkirk; when Medina Sidonia fired his gun to order the fleet to reassemble, few were near enough to hear it.[12] At least for the moment, the discipline of the Armada had been lost.

It was the opportunity Howard had been awaiting. The English commander signalled to attack. About 150 English ships moved in on the Spanish fleet. As they did so the breeze freshened from the north-west and the northerners therefore had both wind and tide running strongly in their favour. Ahead of them, struggling to stay clear of the shoals of Dunkirk, was the *San Martín*. Facing virtually the whole of the English fleet, Medina Sidonia decided to stand and fight to protect his own. Like a wounded bull, he would fight in his *querencia*, and with his four Portuguese galleons in support he moved into the Straits. He dispatched *pataches* to inform those ships that they could find of his predicament and to advise them – unnecessarily, perhaps – to stay clear of the Dunkirk shoals.

In the thick of the main action, Medina Sidonia and Drake came together again as they had at Cadiz in 1587. The English onslaught was ferocious and unremitting, and it was aimed at the ship rather than the men on board: the *San Martín* was struck by over 200 cannon balls on the starboard side, and lost much rigging. Water flooded in, and although the ship was not in danger of sinking, two divers worked all day to patch up the holes as best they could. Probably about forty men were killed. Although much of the fighting was at close quarters – Drake did not give the order to fire until he was within musket range – the Spaniards were in no position to do more than defend themselves and could not have thought of grappling and boarding. But the *San Martín* defended itself valiantly and inflicted significant damage on the *Revenge*. Astonishingly, it was Drake who moved away. He led his ships away in pursuit of the body of the Armada, struggling furiously to stay off the shoals of Dunkirk. Frobisher stayed to fight the *San Martín*, furious once again at what he took to be Drake's cowardice. Hawkins supported him in the *Victory*. But Drake was not fleeing – recognizing that the dreadful damage done to the San Martín had all but disabled it, he moved on to do damage elsewhere.[13] The major galleons rallied to their commander – the ships of Alonso de Leiva, Juan Martínez de Recalde, Oquendo's flagship, the ships of the Spanish and Portuguese *maestres de campo*; Diego Flores de Valdés's flagship, Bertendona's flagship which fought with unrelenting courage; the galleon *San Juan* of Diego Flores's squadron; and the *San Juan de Sicilia* – all these galleons withstood the

The San Lorenzo aground off Calais and the battle of Gravelines, 8 August 1588.

enemy's fire until they had barely any capacity to defend themselves. So close was the action that Medina Sidonia could not see what was going on for the smoke rising around him. During one moment of lucidity, he saw that two Spanish galleons were surrounded by enemy ships and he took the *San Martín* to go to relieve them.

For the *San Lorenzo* the battle would not last long. It lay aground in Calais harbour. The fortress of Calais provided some covering fire for it and Howard ordered some of his small ships to mount a boarding operation. The *San Lorenzo* could offer little resistance, for as it sank into the sand its guns were pointing helplessly towards the sky. Hugo de Moncada was shot through the head – the first commander to die on the Armada. The men who were free to do so fled for the shore. The English pillaged her. The Governor of Calais congratulated the English on their success and claimed the hulk for himself. Howard returned to the fray.[14]

Elsewhere, English artillery effectively prevented the Spanish from grappling. Don Francisco de Toledo attempted to take the *San Felipe* of Portugal to close with the enemy but he was confronted by such firepower from seventeen ships that he could not move forward. Both commanders summoned their fleets to them for the decisive battle. Medina Sidonia ordered *pataches* to take men off the *San Felipe* and the *San Mateo*. The operation succeeded with the *San Mateo* but Diego Pimentel refused to abandon his ship even as it drifted towards the shoals of Zeeland. The *San Felipe* took the men off the hulk *Doncella* but was then itself forced to drift towards Zeeland. Justin of Nassau waited for them. Galleys would have been useful in these dreadful hours. They could have fended the fireships off, manoeuvred the Spanish galleons, protected them.

But the Spanish fought with rare courage. At the end of a terrible day's fighting they had lost only eight ships. 600 or so men perished on 8 August and a further 800 were wounded. This was twice as many as had been killed or wounded in the skirmishes in the Channel. In all a total of 2,636 men were lost in battle – 760 sailors and 1,876 soldiers – just under 10% of the men who had embarked in Lisbon.[15] The ships themselves took a terrible pounding. It was said, not entirely rhetorically, that the bombardment to which they had been subjected was some twenty times more fierce that that of Lepanto.[16] On 9 August, at two o'clock in the morning the wind blew very strongly. The *San Martín* fell away towards the Zeeland coast. Medina Sidonia hoped to be able to re-enter the Channel, still to make his junction with the duke of Parma. It was the eve of St Lawrence's Day. The enemy fleet – still consisting of over 100 ships – was now astern of the Armada. Once again it attacked the *San Martín*. The Spanish defended their flagship and the English moved off. The Spanish fleet was driven strongly towards the shoals. It seemed inevitable that they would be driven on to the shoals where they could be picked off one by one. But then the wind got up. The Armada was driven off into the North Sea. Medina Sidonia ordered all his ships to follow him.

That afternoon the duke summoned his commanders for a council of war to consider their options – should they attempt to return to the Channel, or should they head home around the north of the British Isles? It was unanimously decided that they should try to fight their way back into the Channel if the weather permitted it. But if that was not possible, they had no choice but to head north and round the British Isles. As the wind blew ever more strongly, the *San Martín* led the fleet out into the North Sea. His first priority now to save such of the Armada as he could. The enemy fleet followed him, determined to inflict whatever damage it could. The English stood in disciplined formation, but they too were low on provisions and many of them were running short of cannon balls. The Armada had to find its salvation around the northern coasts of the British Isles. Had they known it, the men who survived the battle of Gravelines still had their worst ordeal ahead of them

The English realized they had won a battle but not necessarily the war; Howard himself recognized what the Armada was still capable of: 'we have chased them in fight until this evening', he wrote on 8 August, 'and distressed them much; but their fleet consisteth of mighty ships and great strength'. More confident of his judgement – as always – Drake realized instinctively that the Armada had failed: 'I hope in God the Prince of Parma and the Duke of Sidonia shall not shake hands this few days; and whensoever they shall meet, I believe neither of them will greatly rejoice of this day's service'.[17]

On 10 August the Armada was underway with a fresh south-west wind and a heavy sea. The enemy was in pursuit. But when the wind dropped in the afternoon the enemy came onto the Spanish rearguard. Medina Sidonia once again led by example, protecting the rearguard. He then led his fleet off into the northern waters. It consisted of 110 ships. He instructed his captains to give as wide a berth as possible to Ireland. The fleet headed north.

On 12 August the English were still close to the Armada but they abandoned the pursuit as they neared Scotland. They knew only too well the horrors that still awaited the Spanish as they journeyed around the British Isles and were themselves in terrible condition, with neither the provisions to feed their men nor the money with which to pay them. Moreover, the injured had to be taken to land. Howard instructed Seymour to stand on duty at the Straits in case Parma tried to cross with the English pursuing the Armada; with great reluctance, he obeyed. He set himself to do what he could for his men. He was sickened and embarrassed by the spectacle that awaited him when he went to inspect his men at Margate: 'Sickness and mortality begins wonderfully to grow amongst us; and it is a most pitiful sight to see, here at Margate, how the men, having no place to receive them into here, die in the streets'. He felt obliged to come ashore himself to lead the effort to provide for them but 'the relief is small that I can provide for them here. It would grieve any man's heart to see them that have served so valiantly to die so miserably'.[18]

Terrible as the situation was on the English ships, it was much worse on the Armada, where the provisions had now been on board for fully three months. On Saturday 12 August, Medina Sidonia ordered that only eight ounces of bread and a half a pint of wine with one pint of water was to be served to each soldier.[19] For five days (13-18 August) the Armada fought its way northwards in the face of squalls and heavy seas. Fog made it impossible to distinguish one ship from another, and the Spanish fleet was therefore divided into several flotillas. On the 19 August, the Armada was again brought together. Ships now began to fall away: the *San Juan de Sicilia* could not be located and the three Levanters were never seen again after 14 August.

'From the 24 August to the 4 September we sailed without knowing whither, through constant storms, fogs, and squalls.' The weather worsened by the day and for a month the Armada was hammered by gales which blew it farther off course and hammered it against the coasts of Scotland and Ireland. It was now that the fleet suffered its heaviest losses. Off the coasts of Scotland and Ireland it lost 6,554 men, many of them slaughtered after they made it to land.[20]

By 3 September Medina Sidonia was delirious with fever He sighted the coast of Spain and on 21 September led eight dreadfully battered galleons into Santander. In the following weeks another forty-three ships made it to Santander. Nine reached San Sebastián and six limped into La Coruña. Of the 127 ships that had left La Coruña in July, ninety-two returned home to Spain. Three were lost in accidents and four in combat. Twenty-eight were lost to the weather.[21]

As the Armada was enduring the worst horrors of the campaign, Philip and his ministers in Madrid were receiving the news that it had in fact triumphed. On 18 August Philip wrote to Medina Sidonia congratulating him on his triumph over 'Drake's armada' and on the following day he wrote to his daughter Catalina Micaela in Savoy that 'my armada has defeated that of England, or some of it'.[22] Three days later, Mateo Vázquez wrote excitedly that 'the most excellent news has come today from the Armada'.[23] On 7 September the Council of War wrote cautiously to Philip that the Armada appeared to have succeeded but it took the precaution of warning him that 'very great victories have (sometimes) been of more harm than profit' and advised him that the news still to come might be bad. When twelve days later the Council heard that the fleet had sailed off into the North Sea it could scarcely bring itself to believe the news. In an agony of uncertainty over the fate of 'our armada' it had to make plans for both offence and defence. Juan de Idiáquez wrote to Parma that the king's agony was greater than could be imagined.[24]

A Spanish naval historian, Capt. Gracia Rivas, has demonstrated that 13,399 men returned to Spanish ports – 3,834 sailors and 9,565 soldiers. Even now, many hundreds died on their ships before they could be brought ashore or in the ports themselves, among them two admirals, Miguel de Oquendo and Juan Martínez de Recalde. Only about half of the ships that were saved could be used again. The Indies trade was dislocated; for nearly three years (October 1586-March 1589) no convoy sailed for Tierra Firme.[25]

Medina Sidonia left Santander on 5 October and arrived home at San Lúcar nineteen days later. Philip commissioned Francisco de Bobadilla to write an assessment of the campaign. Bobadilla gave Medina Sidonia full credit for his leadership. He had done as well as any commander could have done. However, Bobadilla went on to record that 'we found the enemy with a great advantage in ships, better than ours for battle, better designed, with better artillery, gunners and sailors, and so rigged they could handle them and do with them what they wanted. The strength of our Armada was some twenty vessels, and they fought very well, better even than they needed, but the rest fled whenever they saw the enemy attack'. Philip was generous to his commander. He allowed no rebuke to Medina Sidonia to go unanswered and assured him of his enduring favour.[26]

Philip's initial reaction was indeed to vow that he would send another armada at once against England In a singularly revealing statement, he declared that he would 'imperil all his kingdoms in order to punish that wicked woman'. On hearing Zúñiga's report, he insisted (as was reported) 'that he is more than ever determined to follow out his enterprise with all the forces at his disposal', and to put out another fleet in March 1589. In October he vowed that he would if need be sell his own candlesticks to raise money for another fleet. But by the end of October, harsh realities were being absorbed; some advisers were telling Philip that another fleet could not be sent in 1589. Fearful that the English would once again attack Spain as they had done in 1585 and 1587, Philip turned to the Cortes of Castile to raise money to defend Castile itself against invasion.[27] The negotiations were long and hard.

In Flanders, Parma failed to take Bergen-op-Zoom. It was his first major failure. The tide was turning, for it was a portent of more failures in the next years. But Charles-Emmanuel of Savoy took advantage of the weakness of the French crown to invade and conquer the enclave of Saluzzo. More importantly, Henry III assassinated the duke of Guise and his brother the Cardinal. He thereby cut himself off from the Catholic Church that he was nominally defending, united his opponents, and made it possible for Philip to continue to disregard France as a factor in his calculations, for France would again be absorbed by civil wars.[28]

7 After the Armada: Stalemate

The Armada had failed. So much planning had gone into preparing and fighting the campaign that no one had given much thought as to what happened next, but as they absorbed the implications of what had happened, both sides came to realize that everything had changed. The Armada had been designed to solve many problems and its failure meant that most of those problems were now intensified. Most obviously, Philip had sent the Armada to cut out English interference in the affairs of his monarchy, and its failure meant that the English, buoyant with their great victory, would surely now extend and intensify their aggression – in the Low Countries, on the coasts of Iberia and the Atlantic islands of Spain and Portugal, and in the Caribbean. England's Dutch allies felt keenly their own deliverance and were more confident of their ability to confront a power that now seemed far from invincible. Just as keenly, the duke of Parma bitterly regretted the loss of two years campaigning that the Armada had caused him; in 1585 he had seemed truly invincible, but now his reputation had been severely damaged, most especially with his royal master in Spain. The Indies trade had been virtually brought to a halt by the preparations for the Armada and the loss of so many ships now meant that it was difficult to see how it could resume with safety. But the failure of the Armada also meant, as Philip himself was quick to understand, that he would have to send another armada to vindicate himself, his reputation and his power. Elizabeth was exultant, and she entered upon her golden last years as the queen who had saved her country – and much of Protestant Europe – from the Spanish giant. But she remained deeply anxious about Philip's capacity to avenge his failure, about the costs and uncertainties of war, and – above all – about her ability to restrain her sea captains who were convinced now that Spain was terminally weakened and her riches were there to be taken. With her keen sense of financial realities, Elizabeth knew that she did not have the resources to mount a vigorous counter-attack to drive home her advantage and that to do so she would have to enter into arrangements with her sailors and financiers.

Most affected of all by the failure of the Armada was its architect. By the end of 1588 Philip had regained some strength and was once again working hard at his papers but he was never again physically vigorous; he had entered his sixties in 1587 and his last years were marked by increasing physical weakness and ultimately by the dreadful agony of a protracted death.[1] But in one sense he was transformed. The defeat of the Armada was such a bitter blow for him that after 1588 he gambled with ever-increasing recklessness to undo the damage that failure had inflicted upon him. In doing so he made mistake after mistake. In particular, in the years after the Armada he widened rather than restricted the scale of the wars to which he was committed. He determined almost at once to send another armada against England but he also involved himself in the French war of succession and did so by once again relegating the war in the Low Countries to a subsidiary place. He had only one son to succeed him and he raced frenetically against time to secure a settlement that would enable young Philip to succeed to a tolerably favourable situation in Europe.

Philip's advisers shared his perception that he would have to regain his prestige by sending another armada. Indeed, in December 1588 the Council of War urged him to make offensive warfare because it was so much cheaper than defensive. It discussed the formation of a new armada and where it should be sent – Ireland or Wales? It looked for cheap success. It even considered forming a galley fleet in Flanders and sending it to land in Hull in Yorkshire – a place that was not defended and could be surprised.[2]

But Philip had to replace the ships that had been lost in order to defend Spain and the Indies run before he created another armada. He did so with stunning success: in 1589-98 he had over sixty major ships built at the crown's expense and by the time he died in 1598 he was again in command of a fleet which had more than forty galleons at its core. At the heart of the new fleet were the 'Twelve Apostles', ships that were very consciously named to do God's work. These ships were built in the northern dockyards in the years 1588-91. It was now – after the defeat of the great fleet for which he is best known – that Philip actually constructed a royal navy. Indeed in 1594 the fleet was formally named as 'The Royal Fleet of the Ocean Sea', and it operated out of bases in Lisbon, Cadiz and La Coruña to protect the Iberian coasts and to usher home the treasure galleons on the dangerous run from the Azores. Administrative control over the new navy was vested in the *Junta de Galeras*, which had already existed for some time but was now given extended powers over shipbuilding, victualling and provisioning.[3]

The new fleet was paid for by the taxpayers of Castile. In 1590, after extended and difficult negotiations, the Cortes of Castile agreed to provide Philip with 8,000,000 ducats over six years, at 1,333,333 ducats annually. This was a temporary grant, awarded to fight off a threatened invasion of Spain and the money was to be raised by taxes on 'the four species'; of wine, vinegar, olive oil and meat. This was in fact a tax on the essential articles of life. An increase in the *encabezamiento general* raised a further 2,755,555 ducats. The burden on the Castilian taxpayer thereby increased by 4,088,888 ducats annually. The true cost of the armada was found in these taxes.[4] But still the paradox: as Castile sank deeper into penury, treasure flooded in from the Indies; in October 1589 the fleets of New Spain and Peru brought nearly 20,000,000 ducats.[5]

Elizabeth understood well enough that Philip would be obliged to send another armada against her and she certainly understood how close she had

Queen Elizabeth (1533-1603), at St Paul's for the celebration of the victory over the Armada.

come to defeat in the summer of 1588. She therefore decided that the first objective in 1589 was to finish off the Armada veterans as they lay in the harbours of northern Spain. Elizabeth knew that perhaps forty of these ships lay undefended – almost indefensible – in the enormous harbour of Santander and began preparing an expedition to destroy them. Once that had been accomplished, Elizabeth intended that the expedition should proceed to Portugal to provoke a rebellion in favour of Dom Antonio that would concentrate Philip's attentions at home rather than allow him to send another fleet into the Channel. However, Elizabeth did not have the financial resources to mount a major expedition on her own account and to bring it about she had to resort to a joint-stock operation. In the seeds of her financial weakness lay the failure of the expedition, for her partners had priorities that were very different from her own.

Chief among those partners was Francis Drake, and it is likely that from the beginning he had no intention whatsoever of sailing into Santander harbour to destroy the Armada veterans. That would have been comparatively easily done, but tacking out of Santander and working his way along the northern Spanish coast and down to Lisbon was a major undertaking and Drake did not care to risk it. Elizabeth gave Drake permission to station himself off the Azores to intercept the treasure fleet but she insisted that he could do so only after he had accomplished the other two objectives. Most especially – and her instructions were quite explicit – Drake was to do nothing until he had destroyed the Armada veterans. But Drake's eyes were fixed on Spanish silver; for him, the Azores was the priority.

The force that Elizabeth raised was quite large enough for all these purposes, had it taken them singly. The fleet consisted of 180 sail, including twenty Dutch ships, and 23,000 men of whom 19,000 were soldiers. The fleet therefore bore comparison with the Armada of 1588, although there were comparatively few large ships. The soldiers were placed under the command of Sir John Norris, with whom Drake was confident that he could work well. But a third commander appeared, as if from nowhere; Robert Devereux, Earl of Essex, was the dashing new favourite of the queen, and he fled from court to join the expedition and win martial glory for himself. In doing so he disobeyed the queen. It was a poignant augury for the expedition. The fleet sailed from Plymouth on 8 May 1589.

Philip and his ministers had no doubts that the English intended to attack the Armada veterans and they raised such soldiers as they could to defend them, but without any conviction that the men would have either the quality or the numbers to resist the English army. Philip could not have known that in the disobedience of his great enemy would lie his own salvation. Drake sailed not to Santander but to La Coruña. He did so because he claimed that he had information that a number of Armada ships were taking shelter there. In fact, the port was almost empty of important ships. Drake spent a fortnight sacking the town, as if it was still 1585 and he had no greater purpose than to provoke

Philip II's anger. He achieved nothing, and the Spanish lost only one Armada veteran, the *San Juan*, destroyed by its own crew to prevent it falling into English hands. Drake had wasted a fortnight – and a fortnight's victuals for his enormous force – and to no real purpose. And at Lisbon and in the Azores, Spanish forces were put on war footing: Drake would have no element of surprise on this expedition.

The fleet moved down the Iberian coast and Drake landed Norris and his men at Peniche, 80km north of Lisbon. But the presence (and preparedness) of the Spanish army ensured that the Portuguese dared not rise in support of the invader and Norris was allowed to press on, virtually unhindered, to Lisbon. The defences were well-prepared and the English mounted only a token assault on the walls before retreating back toward Drake and his ships. The Earl of Essex threw a spear against the walls of Lisbon, as his sole military action of the engagement. But the cost of the spurious little campaign was extreme: Norris lost 2,000 men to heat and exhaustion.

Drake now sought to justify himself by achieving the third objective that Elizabeth had set out for him – to take the treasure fleet at the Azores. But Drake's fleet was hit by a storm off Portugal and only with difficulty did it even make its way to Vigo. Drake burned parts of the town and then attempted to sail to the Azores to catch the treasure fleet. But he could make little headway against the winds and had to turn for home. The condition of his men was now truly dreadful and they were dying by their hundreds every day. When Drake reached Plymouth at the end of June perhaps as many as 11,000 of his men were dead. These losses were comparable with those on the Armada itself and they had brought no financial or strategic gain to England. Drake had failed, humiliatingly and almost totally. He had betrayed the trust of the Queen and instead of crippling Spain's naval recovery he had allowed it to proceed apace. Elizabeth was furious and did not allow Drake to sail again on her service until 1595. The blow that should have been struck against the Armada veterans went unstruck.[6]

The great expedition had been as singular a failure as had the Armada itself. Smaller expeditions were much more successful. In the years 1589-91, no fewer than 236 English ships launched attacks upon Spanish and Portuguese ships wherever they could find them in European and American waters. The Indies trade was severely restricted while the Azores swarmed with English ships waiting for the treasure ships when they did manage to return.[7] In 1590 only twelve ships sailed for Spain from the Caribbean and in 1591 the departure of the treasure fleet for Spain was held up by the authorities' fears that Hawkins and John Frobisher might attack it; seventy-seven ships were prepared to leave Havana in July 1591 but so fearful were the authorities of the English that for the first time they despatched the treasure not in the traditional convoy but in fast frigates (*gallizabras*) which crossed the Atlantic without stopping at the Azores, arriving home early in 1592. In 1592 itself only nine ships sailed to Spain – the smallest home-bound fleet in the history of the

Indies trade. The Indies trade was grinding to a halt. Here indeed was a major success for the English, the vindication of all that they had learned about fighting the Spaniards – small fleets, rapid engagement, quick departures. But not all was triumph for the English. In 1591 a squadron led by Lord Thomas Howard was surprised by Don Alonso de Bazán off Flores in the Azores; Howard had six of the queen's galleons and managed to get all but one of them away. The *Revenge*, commanded by Sir Richard Greville, fought for fifteen hours against Bazán's squadron of fifteen ships; it was heroic fight which passed into national folklore, but it was not very intelligently managed – when the ship surrendered, only eight of its seventy-eight barrels of gunpowder had been used. Greville had fought a Spanish squadron with muskets for the best part of the engagement. The Spanish arrived back home with what they described as the finest battery of brass guns on the ocean.[8]

Philip could not concentrate solely on the English and their ships, for in the years after the Armada affairs in France reached their supreme crisis, and in Philip's eyes came to be of greater importance even than English affairs. The murder of the Guise brothers destroyed the credibility of Henry III in the eyes of the Catholic Church. The pope summoned Henry to Rome to account for the murder of a prince of the Church – a summons which he naturally ignored – and the Sorbonne condemned him as a tyrant (7 January 1589) and thereby validated assassination attempts on him. City after city across France joined the Catholic League – Rouen, Dijon, Orleans, Toulouse and Marseilles. Faced with the loss of Catholic France, Henry III allied himself with Henry of Navarre (Treaty of Plessis-les-Tours, 30 April 1589) but on 1 August, as he was preparing to go to war with his Huguenot partner, he was assassinated. In his last moments, Henry declared Henry of Navarre to be his legitimate heir. One year to the day after the Armada reached the Channel, France had a Protestant monarch. Philip II quickly decided to make it his chief priority in foreign affairs to prevent the succession of Henry of Navarre to the French throne. It was perhaps the most important single decision that he took in his reign. Now, the campaigns in the Low Countries and the war against England at sea would be of secondary importance. A year after he had bent all the resources of his monarchy to defeat Elizabeth, Philip decided that the war against her was of secondary importance to that against Henry of Navarre in France.

Philip's decision came against the backcloth of a desultory campaign by Parma in the Low Countries, the expression of the great general's realization that he could not recapture former glories in the war. Realizing how strong the Dutch were becoming, and how a multiplicity of wars was weakening Spanish power, Parma urged Philip to seek a negotiated settlement with Holland and Zeeland. Philip initially rejected the advice but by the time he changed his mind it was too late, for the Dutch were now in the ascendant.[9] As Parma despaired, the Dutch, under Maurice of Nassau, son of William of Orange, made great progress and recovered many of the towns that Parma had taken in the early 1580s.

In France, Henry of Navarre realized that he could never win the throne unless he converted to Roman Catholicism; although he never actually said it, he understood full well that 'Paris was worth a mass'. On 4 August 1589 he indicated that he would convert to Catholicism.[10] Anxious that France was now being lost to him by Henry's conversion, Philip determined to put forward the candidature of his daughter Isabella Clara Eugenia to the throne as the granddaughter of Henry II. However, women were barred by law from succeeding to the French throne and Isabella's candidature served only to remind many French Catholics that Philip's was a foreign cause. It also drew in foreign support: the fear that Spain might succeed on land in France where she had failed on sea against her, encouraged Elizabeth to send 3,600 men to Normandy in September 1589.[11]

On 14 March 1590 Henry won the battle of Ivry and opened the road to Paris. Philip decided that Paris had to be saved and ordered Parma into France. Parma protested but had to obey and in August 1590 led 17,000 men into France. He relieved Paris in September and then left France against Philip's orders. His brilliant success did not compensate him for the loss of yet another campaigning season in the Low Countries.

In October 1590 Philip opened yet another front, by sending a galley fleet to Brittany, establishing a base at Blavet on the southern coast of Brittany. Spain now had a base at the southern end of the Channel. It would not serve for the galleons but might, in conjunction with the ports held by Parma serve to bring the whole of the northern French coast under Spanish control. This would in turn open the possibility of the Spanish making use of the ports of northern France to mount an invasion of England. Elizabeth sent 3,000 men under Norris to Brittany and 4,000 under Essex to Normandy. They achieved little more than to tie down the Spanish forces but in the circumstances that was enough. The war between England and Spain was now a land war fought for the future of France.[12]

In 1591 Maurice of Nassau took Zutphen and Deventer while Henry IV took Chartres and Noyon and in November besieged Rouen. The threat to Normandy, to Paris and to Parma's southern flank was very real. Philip ordered Parma into France yet again. Once again, Parma objected; once again, he had to obey. At the beginning of 1592 he marched into France, with 18,000 men. He relieved Rouen and retreated towards the Netherlands. However, he was wounded in the arm and lost a great deal of blood (24 April). He reached the Low Countries 'more dead than alive' and never recovered. He died on the night of 2-3 December, at forty-seven years of age. He was the most brilliant of Philip's servants, and it was characteristic of Philip's distrust of him that when Parma died he was on the point of being dismissed from his command.[13]

On 25 July 1593 Henry IV announced his conversion to Catholicism. While his Huguenot supporters were dismayed by his apostasy, Philip II was devastated, for he now lost his justification for interfering in France. Henry

Maurice of Nassau, Prince of Orange (1567-1625).

was crowned king of France at Chartres on 27 February 1594 and shortly afterwards entered Paris without meeting opposition. France was united again, and for the first time since 1559 went formally to war with Spain: Henry declared war on 17 January 1595, denouncing Philip's interference in French affairs and presenting himself as a national leader and conciliator. He justified his pretensions by briskly marching down to Burgundy to defeat an invading

Pedro Enríquez de Acevedo, Count of Fuentes (c.1530-1610).

Spanish army at the battle of Fontaine-Francaise (June 1595). On 20 September, the duke of Mayenne, last of the Guise brothers, concluded a truce with the king. The Catholic League was disintegrating. At the same time the English helped inflict a major defeat on the Spanish in Brittany by conquering the fort of Crozon and massacring its garrison. The Spanish would not control the northern French ports and use them to mount an invasion of England.

151

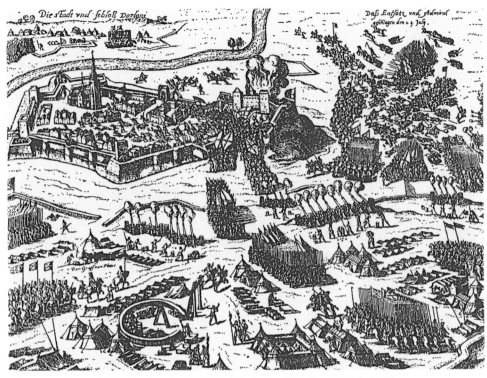

A Spanish victory in the 1590s: The battle of Doullens (24 July 1595).

Having lost the war for the French succession, Philip began once again to consider the possibility of dealing with England by sending an armada against her.

On the face of it he had the resources. No fleets had arrived in Spain in 1594 because of fears of English corsairs and so two fleets arrived in April-May 1595, bringing 22,000,000 ducats of which about 7,000,000 were for the crown. A further 8,000,000 ducats arrived in September, but even this unexampled wealth was not enough for Philip's wars, for he was spending 10,000,000 ducats annually on his military budgets alone, twice as much as he had done twenty years earlier. In 1580 the kingdom of Castile had supported 20,000 men but in 1598 it was 50,000.[14]

This burden of war – of unsuccessful wars fought abroad but paid for at home – could not be borne much longer, and the 1590s saw growing criticism of Philip and his policies. The Cortes of 1592-98 lasted twice as long as any of its predecessors as it wrangled bitterly with the ministers of the crown over the king's demands for monies for his foreign wars. In October 1591 eight leaflets were posted on prominent buildings in Avila criticizing the 'greed and tyranny' of the king. The government was panicked, fearing that Castile was about to follow Aragon into rebellion; Don Diego de Bracamonte, a nobleman, went to the scaffold on 17 February 1592 as a warning to the nobility of Castile not to

The Archduke Albert of Austria (1559-1621).

153

involve themselves in criticism of their king and his strategy. Other opposition was less formal; in May 1590 the Inquisition arrested Lucrecia de León, a twenty-one year old women who was given to prophecy. She had prophesied before the Armada left that it would sail off into northern waters, and when she now castigated Philip as a tyrant who was 'responsible for the evil and ruin of Spain' and his senior ministers as men who were 'involved in dirty and abominable things' the government had to act. Lucrecia was brought before the Inquisition. The investigation lasted for five years before a lenient verdict was handed down.[15]

Philip appointed his nephew, the Archduke Albert, to be Governor and Captain General in the Low Countries. Albert immediately proved his mettle: on 27 April he took Calais and put the garrison to the sword. The Spanish had a port, although not a deep-water one. At court in London, Elizabeth could hear Albert's guns assaulting Calais and she decided to re-engage with Spain at sea. She determined on a two-pronged attack: Drake (redeemed from his disgrace thanks to the support of Essex) would sail once again to the Caribbean on a semi-private expedition while the Royal Navy – under the Lord Admiral himself, Lord Howard – would imitate Drake's great attack of 1587 in Cadiz in an attempt to damage Philip's re-emergent naval strength. Two English fleets prepared to strike at Spain and her empire.

Drake sailed on 17 September 1595 with twenty-seven ships, including six of the Queen's galleons. It was hoped that at the least he might seize a treasure ship or two and that at best he might even establish a base from which English ships could operate within the Caribbean. He was under orders to return by the early summer of 1596 to help defence against a second armada. Reluctantly, he took Sir John Hawkins with him; Elizabeth had paid for two-thirds of the cost of the expedition and it is probable that she insisted that Hawkins accompany Drake to keep an eye on him. The two men thus sailed together in the Caribbean for the first time since 1568, and they died together, both of them from disease rather than from enemy action – Hawkins died off Puerto Rico (12 November 1595) and Drake off Puerto Bello (28 January 1596). It was a poignant end to two great careers. The Spanish general commanding the defence against Drake, Don Alonso de Sotomayor, paid generous tribute to Drake – 'one of the most famous men of his profession that have existed in the world, very courteous and honourable with those who have surrendered, of great humanity and gentleness, virtues which must be praised even in an enemy'. [16]Philip was less generous: he was enervated by the news of Drake's death and it was noted that he 'shows the keenest delight and declares that this good news will help him to get well rapidly'.[17]

Howard arrived off Cadiz on 29 June with 120 sail. He had seventeen royal galleons with him, among them the *Ark Royal* and the *Dreadnought*. This, therefore, was a major royal expedition. It was also an international one, for Howard had a Dutch squadron with him. The fleet sailed with discipline befitting its status; not until it was off the Spanish coast was its purpose

The burial of Drake.

revealed to the captains. In the harbour at Cadiz it found no fewer than sixty ships, half of them galleons fully laden with their cargoes for the voyage to the Indies. There were also six royal galleons to escort them and fifteen galleys to defend the port. Howard moved in quickly on the galleons; he destroyed two 'Apostles' (the *San Felipe* and the *Santo Tomás*) and captured two more (the *San Mateo* and the *San Andrés*). However, he made the mistake of allowing the Spanish to negotiate with him for the merchantmen. As discussions dragged on, the Spanish burned thirty of their finest merchantmen with their fabulous cargoes rather than yield them to the English. Essex led the assault on Cadiz and held it for nearly two weeks. It may have been his intention to establish a garrison in Cadiz to prevent the Spanish from using it. This, however, was unrealistic and Howard insisted on leading the whole force back out to sea. Essex was furious, and it was small consolation to him that he left behind him a city that was seriously damaged. Medina Sidonia himself marched troops to the defence of Cadiz but was unable to do anything to restrict the damage. Howard had inflicted substantial damage on Philip's revived navy and he arrived home, triumphant, docking in Plymouth on 18 August. He believed that he had won a victory even greater than that of 1588, for he had devastated the enemy in his chief seaport.

Elizabeth was initially thrilled by the reports of the triumph: 'let the army know I care not so much for being Queen that I am sovereign of such subjects'. However, when she came to realize how much plunder had been stolen from her by her own soldiers and sailors and – more especially – when she came to appreciate the value that had been lost when the merchantmen had gone up in smoke she was furious. Once again, her precious money had been wasted, once again her commanders had failed to carry out her orders. The expedition had been a failure as far as the queen was concerned and the news that the treasure fleet had arrived at San Lúcar on 27 September with 12,000,000 ducats'-worth of silver only increased her rage.[18]

Elizabeth's anger was nothing compared to Philip's. The attack on Cadiz was the greatest humiliation of his reign. For two weeks an enemy force comprised of heretics had despoiled his most important seaport and destroyed some of his most valuable and prized galleons without any significant response having been made. Once again the Indies trade was brought to a halt; not until February 1598 did the next Indies fleet return to Seville. Philip decided almost instantly that he would seek his revenge by sending the second armada against Elizabeth.

The second armada would sail – as perhaps the first should have done – to Ireland. A rebellion had broken out under Hugo O'Neill, earl of Tyrone, and Elizabeth viewed it with such seriousness that in February 1595 she withdrew her troops from Brittany to deal with it. Philip decided to exploit Elizabeth's difficulties exactly as she had exploited his in the Low Countries; the prospect appealed greatly to him. As his commander he chose Don Martín de Padilla y Manrique, hereditary *Adelantado Mayor* of Castile. The *Adelantado* was experienced in many theatres of war. He had fought at St Quentin in 1557, at the Alpujarras in 1568 and at Lepanto in 1571. In 1585 he had been appointed Captain General of the Galleys of Spain. He was another of the soldiers who were ennobled by Philip II, having been raised to the countship of Santa Gadea in 1587. He had fought against the English at Lisbon in 1589 and in 1596 was appointed Captain General of the Atlantic Fleet. But if he had held important naval commands, as Medina Sidonia had not, he was much inferior to his predecessor as an organizer. Not the least of his difficulties in coordinating the work of others was that he had an unfailing ability to fall out with everybody with whom he worked. The *Adelantado* was an abrasive and tactless man, easy to insult others, quick to take offence himself.

In a very real sense, the *Adelantado's* appointment to command the second armada was accidental, for he had been sent to Lisbon in July 1596 to reassure the people of the city that they would be defended if the English followed up their assault on Cadiz with an attack upon Lisbon. In practice, his mission was to see to it that no rising took place to support Dom Antonio. As part of doing so, he sequestered some Dutch ships that were at anchor in Lisbon.

Philip decided during October that he would proceed with his second armada. As he had done in 1588, he ordered that prayers be said throughout Spain for his intentions (without specifying what they were) and gave instructions that the fleet be prepared to sail. In fact, it was not remotely

Philip II, Juan Pantoja de la Cruz.

ready for its mission and – as Medina Sidonia had done in 1588 – the *Adelantado* had his captains sign a memorial to the king urging him to be patient while the fleet was properly prepared. As in 1588, Philip again insisted that the fleet sail.

One lesson was learned from 1588: the fleet was taken from Lisbon to Ferrol to shorten its journey. ninety-eight ships were assembled at Ferrol, twenty-seven of them royal galleons. They had about 15,000 men on board. As in 1588 the fleet could barely sail out of harbour; the *Adelantado* had to make four attempts before he could leave the harbour (16 October). Predictably, the fleet then sailed into a great autumnal storm: off Cape Finisterre on 20 October, seven galleons, twenty-five larger merchantmen and many smaller craft were lost. 2,000 men perished. The fleet returned to Ferrol. Philip insisted that it sail for England, but it was in no condition even to attempt to do so. The English made very extensive preparations to receive the *Adelantado*, and it was some weeks before they heard what had happened and were able to stand their men down.[19]

The failure of the second armada was deeply wounding to Philip. Once again he suffered a physical collapse, in agony now with bowel trouble and loss of sleep. Even his closest advisers urged him now to seek a settlement and to bring the war with England to an end: the Council of State itself reminded him that wars were only fought in order to win the peace.[20] But as the silver flooded in from the Indies Philip decided to risk one last gamble; in 1596, two fleets reached Spain, bringing with them 15,000,000 ducats of silver. It was the truest expression of Philip's failure to match income against expenditure, ambition against reality, that the crown now had to declare another suspension of payments – the fourth of the reign (November 1596). The Council of Finance estimated that the shortfall in its income for 1597 would be 7,000,000 ducats and that it was some 25,000,000 ducats short of its needs for the years 1596-9. There was no income now from the *millones*, which had expired in 1596.[21]

The financial crisis meant that no effective campaign could be funded in the Low Countries. But the temptation to send a third armada was encouraged by the news that Elizabeth was preparing yet another major expedition to attack Spain, this time under the earl of Essex himself, the chief advocate of a belligerent prosecution of the war. Elizabeth signed the Treaty of Greenwich (24 May 1596) with Henry IV as a mutual defensive and offensive treaty against Spain. In October the United Provinces joined the alliance.

Once again, Philip vested command in the *Adelantado*. He was ordered to seize Falmouth and then to intercept Essex's fleet as it returned from the Azores – the Spanish would be waiting in the Channel for the English! The fleet was larger than those of 1588 or 1596: it consisted of 136 ships, of which forty-four were royal galleons. It carried 12,634 men. Familiar patterns recurred: Philip harried his commander to ensure that he sailed even though they insisted that the fleet was neither adequate nor prepared and the fleet left

The surviving children of Philip II: 1. Philip III, King of Spain (1598-1621).

The surviving children of Philip II: 2. Isabella Clara Eugenia (1566-1633).

very late in the year (18 October). This time, however, progress was good until the fleet reached the Channel. As the fleet approached the Lizard, a storm blew up which dispersed the fleet. The *Adelantado* could only see three ships around him and so he had to order the return home. Over the next two weeks 108 ships returned to the ports of north-west Spain. The number of ships lost was comparatively small, but they included two more 'Apostles' – the *San Bartolomé* and the *San Lucás*, both of which sank. In 1596-7, therefore, Philip lost six of his twelve 'Apostles'. His navy was suffering catastrophic losses even as he was rebuilding it. For all that, the *Adelantado* had come close to success, for he had arrived off the English coast to find that fourteen of England's twenty-six major fighting ships were away, off the Azores. The English admiral William Monson noted that Spain had 'never had so dangerous an enterprise upon us'. But God's winds were Protestant.[22]

Essex's voyage was as unsuccessful as the *Adelantado's*. Essex set out to achieve a number of objectives – to destroy Spanish naval power; to capture the treasure fleet; and then to attack the West Indies. In reality, Essex's purposes were domestic, designed to consolidate his position at court with a brilliant success against the Spanish. But he too found it difficult to get out of port and only made it out of Plymouth at the second attempt (27 August). He ran into another storm in the Bay of Biscay and decided to abandon his attempt on Ferrol in order to catch the treasure fleet at the Azores. He missed the fleet and headed for home. By 31 October he had dismissed his men.

The Indies fleet brought 7,000,000 ducats of silver but even Philip had to recognize that he had now to bring at least some of his wars to a halt. He ended with war with France by the Peace of Vervins (2 May 1598). France was now the equal of Spain. The United Provinces and England would have to fight on without French support. Four days later Philip renounced the Low Countries to Isabella as her dowry for her marriage to Albert. This too was a restatement of the conditions under which he had begun his reign, repeating almost exactly the terms laid down in his father's abdication of 1555. Isabella and Albert would be able to fight the war in the Low Countries from their local base. But Spain retained five major fortresses, financial control over the war and leadership of the Army of Flanders. The devolution of authority was cosmetic and insubstantial. It was deeply resented by the Spanish commanders such as Fuentes, who thought it another abdication. They determined to undermine Albert and all that he stood for.

The settlements of May 1598 recognized the failure of the aggressive foreign policy that Philip had pursued for fifteen years. Philip left for the Escorial on 1 July 1598. He took to his bed on 22 July, never to rise from it. In fulminating pain he stoically endured his last agonies. He died on 13 September 1598. He could not have known it, but in his last dreadful agony his government received reports that English ships had appeared off Ibiza, and it was noted that 'they have begun to make themselves felt' in the Mediterranean. He had risked so much to stop English ships sailing into his possessions and now as he lay dying they were sailing into the inland sea itself. The naval war against England was now encompassing the whole of the Iberian coast.[23]

Conclusion

The Armada was a great and historic event. It was a crucial part of what has rightly been called 'the first world war', a conflict which stretched across the face of the globe as English seapower searched out the weak points of Spain's imperial power in Europe, the Atlantic and even in the Pacific.[1] It was also the first naval war in modern times which was fought outside the Mediterranean or the Baltic.[2] In the history of warfare, therefore, the campaign has an important role. Of course, it was also central to many of the issues involved in the political development of the nation-states of western Europe and to the balances between and within them. Clearly, the immediate futures of Spain and of England hung on the outcome, but so too did those of many of the countries of western Europe. In bringing his great power to bear in the attack on England, Philip inadvertently helped to bring about a balancing of power in Europe as small nations combined to fight him off. The failure of the fleet had profound implications for the development of Christianity in Europe, for the division of the continent into a Catholic south and a Protestant north.

At a personal level, the Armada campaign helped to make national heroes of Elizabeth and of Drake while Philip is often remembered now chiefly for the failure of the fleet and Medina Sidonia is remembered only because of it. But for some men the campaign marked a beginning rather than an end, for several veterans came to exercise crucial roles at the centre of government. This was most notably true of the Spanish: Pedroso, Bobadilla, Mexía, Pimentel and Zúñiga all became key policymakers under Philip III, and Mexía and Zúñiga in particular played determinant roles in the development of Spanish foreign policy into the 1620s. Both men learned from the Armada campaign that Spain had to fight wars on land against her opponents in northern Europe, but they also learned that Spain must never again commit everything to a single throw of the die at sea and that she had to maintain a fleet in northern waters – what became the 'Armada of Flanders'.[3] It was central to their polity that Spain should maintain peace with England. This was most fully expressed by Mexía himself at the Council of State in 1614 when he eloquently advised Philip III to maintain peace with England above all other priorities because Spain simply could not afford the expenses of fighting against English seapower. Mexía had learned the true lesson of the Armada for Spanish policymakers, and it was to restate the principle that Isabella the Catholic had laid down at the very beginning of the Spanish empire – 'Peace with England at all costs because of the Indies'.[4]

The history of 'the Armada' has also been significant in the way in which the nations involved have regarded themselves. Until very recently the history of

The Armada in History: 1. The Marquis of Santa Cruz: a celebratory medal, 1988.

the Armada was an Anglo-Saxon history and it contributed to a view of English history that has had powerful and often negative impact upon the way in which the English have regarded themselves. In this view Philip II became the precursor of several continental dictators whose designs for European hegemony were thwarted only by the gallantry and self-sacrifice of the island race. Conversely, Spanish self-perception has often been coloured by the failure of the great expedition, which has become the symbol of the decline of Spanish power in Europe. The Armada deserved a better history than this, and in recent years it has had it as scholars, both Spanish and English, have addressed themselves to the real issues in the tumultuous campaign. In doing so they have redefined the significance of the campaign in its time and in ours. For nearly a century Spain's power in Europe and the world had grown insistently, but in 1588 that growth was arrested and although Spain remained the first power of Europe for a further fifty years after 1588 her power was

Opposite page: The Armada in History: 2. The memorial at Plymouth Hoe.

never again considered to be unchallengeable. It was perhaps as an expression of this that when peace was made to bring the war to an end, the Spanish minister, the Constable of Castile, had to travel to London to negotiate. When the peace was ratified, no less a figure than Effingham came to Spain to witness the swearing of the treaty. Medina Sidonia was conspicuously absent. A new era had begun and during the discussions in Madrid the proposal was put forward for a Spanish Marriage to seal the renewed amity between the two nations. But as England and Spain renewed their traditional friendship, policymakers in both nations knew that everything had changed.

Notes

1 England, Philip of Spain and the daughters of Henry VIII

1 *CSPS* xiii, 11.
2 Rodríguez-Salgado, *Changing Face of Empire*, pp. 79-92.
3 *CSPS* xiii, 7, 30.
4 Scarisbrick, *Henry VIII*, pp. 201-4.
5 Macaffrey, *Elizabeth I*, pp. 12-29.
6 Loades, *Mary Tudor*, pp. 234, 248.
7 Rodríguez-Salgado, *Changing Face of Empire*, pp. 101-34.
8 Guy, *Tudor England*, p. 248.
9 *CSPS* xiii, 336, 502; Feria to Philip, London, 14 and 29 Dec. 1558, copies, Archivo General de Simancas [AGS] Estado [E] 811, ff. 99 and 105; Rodríguez-Salgado, *Changing Face of Empire*, pp. 315-28.
10 Garrisson, *Sixteenth-Century France*, pp. 256-78.
11 Macaffrey, *Elizabeth I*, pp. 5-7.
12 Ibid., p. 49.
13 On Elizabeth and her ministers, Smith, *Emergence of a Nation State*, pp. 114-26.
14 Macaffrey, *Elizabeth I*, pp. 8-9.
15 Smith, *Emergence of a Nation State*, p. 115; Guy, *Tudor England*, p. 280.
16 Macaffrey, *Elizabeth I*, pp. 48-59.

2 The Spanish Monarchy

1 Braudel, *Mediterranean World*, ii, pp. 476-517 and 675-8.
2 F. Ruiz Martin, 'La Población española al comienzo de los tiempos modernos', *Cuadernos de Historia*, i (Madrid : 1967), p. 199.
3 Lovett, *Early Habsburg Spain*, pp. 101-24.
4 Bakewell, *Latin America*, pp. 34-9.
5 Hoffman, *The Spanish Crown and the Defense of the Caribbean*, passim; Lovett, *Early Habsburg Spain*, pp. 83-97.

6 Padmore, *Maritime Supremacy*, p. 8.

7 Boxer, *Portuguese Seaborne Empire*, pp. 39-65 and 207-29.

8 J. Lynch, *Spain 1516-1598 from nation state to world empire* (Oxford, 1991), p. 236.

9 Parker, *Dutch Revolt*, pp. 19-67.

10 J. L. González Novalín, *El Inquisidor Fernando de Valdés (1483-1568)*, ii (Oviedo : 1971), pp. 233-35.

11 Maltby, W. *The Black Legend in England. The development of anti-Spanish sentiment, 1558-1660 (Duke Univ. Press, 1971), p. ..*

12 Braudel, *Mediterranean World*, pp. 960-66.

13 A. W. Lovett, 'Juan de Ovando and the Council of Finance (1573-1575), The Historical Journal, [HJ], XV, 1 (1972), p. 7.

14 Checa, *Felipe II*, esp. pp. 76-85.

15 Boyden, *The Courtier and the King*, pp. 105-11, and W. Maltby, *Alba : A Biography of Fernando Álvarez de Toledo, Third Duke of Alba, 1507-1582, pp. 86-109.(Berkeley, 1983)*, pp. 29-43.

16 Thompson, *War and Government*, p. 16.

17 *CSPS* xiv, 342.

3 Breakdown : The Queen of Scots, the Privateer and the Iron Duke

1 On Elizabeth and Mary, Macaffrey, *Elizabeth I*, pp. 103-44.

2 Lyon, *Menéndez de Avilés*, pp. 3-29 and 61-72.

3 'Relación de los Nauios que dizen q[ue] van a las Indias', and Guzmán de Silva to Philip II, London, 11 July 1567, AGS E 816, ff. 48 and 106.

4 'The third troublesome voyage made by the *Jesus of Lubeck*', *Hakluyt's Voyages*, pp. 397-405 and Cummins, *Drake*, p. 28.

5 '*Letters from the Woods of Segovia*', the *Compromise* and the *Request* printed by Kossman and Mellink, *Texts*, nos. 1, 3, 4.

6 Ibid., no. 6, quotation at p. 74; a map of iconoclastic riots, Parker, *Dutch Revolt*, p. 77.

7 Parker, *Dutch Revolt*, pp. 90-101.

8 De Espes to Alba, London, 30 Dec. 1568, AGS E 820, fol. 127.

9 *BMO*, no. 18; *CSPS II Eliz.* nos. 80, 87.

10 *BMO*, no. 22.

11 Ibid., no. 28.

12 Ibid., no. 25.

13 Macaffrey, *Elizabeth I*, p. 128.

14 *BMO*. no. 25; *CSPS II Eliz.*, 165.

15 Macaffrey, *Elizabeth I*, pp. 134-44.

16 Rodger, *The Safeguard of the Sea*, p. 238.

17 Parker, *Dutch Revolt*, pp. 138-42.

18 Parker, *Army of Flanders*, pp. 139-42 and 287.

19 A. W. Lovett, 'A new governor for the Netherlands : the appointment of Don Luis de Requesens, Comendador Mayor de Castilla', *European Studies Review*, 1971, 1, no. 2, pp. 89-103; Pi Corrales, *España y las potencias nórdicas*, p. 81.

20 Parker, *Army of Flanders*, pp. 232-4 and 271-2.

21 Pi Corrales, *España y las potencias nórdicas*, pp. 105-6.

22 Ibid., p. 89, n. 1.

23 *BMO*, 62.

24 Ibid., 73, 76, 78; Pi Corrales, *España y las potencias nórdicas*, pp. 167-8.

25 Rodger, *The Safeguard of the Sea*, pp. 221—37.

26 Ibid., pp. 213-15.

27 Parker, 'The Dreadnought Revolution', p. 224.

28 *SW*, pp. 270-2.

29 George Gascoigne, 'The Spoyle of Antwerpe', (London ? : 1576).

30 *BMO*, 90.

31 Ibid., 93.

32 Rodger, *The Safeguard of the Sea*, pp. 244-5.

33 *BMO*, no. 117; see also 108-31 and 146-7.

4 War and Peace : 1580 – 5

1 Morineau, *Incroyables gazettes*, pp. 72-4.

2 Cerezo Martínez, *Las Armadas de Felipe II*, pp. 288-9; Casado Soto, *Los Barcos Españoles del Siglo XVI*, pp. 45-6; Maltby, *Alba*, pp. 283-305.

3 Lynch, *Spain 1516-1598*, p. 435.

4 'Resolución del tanteo ... del dinero ... para los gastos desta Jornada de portugal', Lisbon, 22 April 1582, AGS Guerra Antigua [GA] 140, f. 69 and *asientos* with the Fuggers, ibid., ff. 1-22.

5 Fernández Duro, *La Conquista de las Azores en 1583*, pp. 11-17; *CSPV* viii, 49; Cerezo Martínez, *Las Armadas de Felipe II*, pp. 291-2.

6 *BMO.*, 332, 340; AGS GA 139, ff. 200, 210, 230; *CSPV* viii, 95, 103.

7 *BMO.*, 340.

8 Casado Soto, *Los Barcos Españoles del Siglo XVI*, pp. 45-51; Thompson, *War and Government*, pp. 32-3; Goodman, *Spanish Naval Power*, p. 3.

9 *BMO*, 379, 380.

10 Ibid., 395

11 Parker, *Dutch Revolt*, pp. 194-8.

12 Wernham, *Before the Armada*, p. 360.

13 Rodger, *The Safeguard of the Sea*, p. 246.

14 *BMO*, 305.

15 Ibid., 328.

16 Parker, *Dutch Revolt*, p. 207.

17 Garrisson, *Sixteenth Century France*, pp. 307-16.

18 Wernham, *Before the Armada*, pp. 340, 381; Rodger, *The Safeguard of the Sea*, p. 249.

19 E. Cock, 'Anales del Año Ochenta y Cinco', in García Mercadal (ed.), *Viajes de Extranjeros*, ii, pp. 1293-1412.

20 R. Villari, *The Revolt of Naples* (Cambridge : 1993), pp. 19-55.

21 *BMO*, 411, 415, 416; Rodger, *Safeguard of the Sea*, p. 249.

22 *BMO.*, 411; S. Adams, 'The Outbreak of the Elizabethan Naval War against the Spanish Empire : The Embargo of May 1585 and Sir Francis Drake's West Indies Voyage', in Rodríguez-Salgado and Adams, *England, Spain and the Gran Armada*, pp. 45-69; Cummins, *Drake*, pp. 132-4 and Kelsey, *Drake*, p. 241.

23 *BMO.*, 483.

24 *CSPV* viii, 284; Van der Essen, *Farnèse*, iv, pp. 136-7.

25 Wernham, *Before the Armada*, pp. 371-2.

26 Rodger, *The Safeguard of the Sea*, p. 248.

27 Kelsey, *Drake*, pp. 240-79.

28 *BMO*, 480, 485, 487, 494.

29 Ibid., 493.

30 *SW.*, 59.

31 Minute of Council of State, 20 Jan. 1588, AGS E 2855, no fol.

5 Plans, Preparations and Providence

1 *BMO.*, 498.

2 Parker, *Grand Strategy*, pp.209-28.

3 I. A. A. Thompson, 'Spanish Armada Guns', *War and Society in Habsburg Spain*, p. 370. See also Martin and Parker, *Spanish Armada*, pp. 195-225.

4 *BMO*, 503, 511.

5 Ibid., 2449; *CSPV* iv, 133.

6 Garrisson, *Sixteenth-Century France*, pp. 378-9.

7 *BMO*, 518.

8 SW, pp. 61-4.

9 *BMO.*, 571, 599.

10 Ibid., 661, 671, 688, 689, 727, 1200.

11 *SW.*, pp. 107-9.

12 *BMO.*, 2352, 2379.

13 Ibid., 2840; HO. pp. 33-7; Chaunu, *Séville et l'Atlantique, 1504-1650*, VI/I, pp. 127-32

14 Thompson, 'The Invincible Armada', pp. 5-6.

15 *CSPS Eliz iv*, 193.

16 Ibid., 198.

17 Ibid., 209.

18 Ibid., 210.

19 *BMO.*, 4134, 4144.

20 *CSPS Eliz. iv*, 223, 242.

21 Ibid., 239, 244, 246.

22 Ibid., 251.

23 Rodger, *The Safeguard of the Sea*, pp. 268-9.

24 *CSPS Eliz. iv*, 252.

25 Ibid., 253.

26 Ibid., 264.

27 Ibid., 278.

28 Ibid., 250.

29 Ibid., 226, 254, 255, 261.

30 Ibid., 271

31 Ibid., 287, 288.

32 Ibid., 294.

33 Ibid., 217, 272; *DSA*. i, pp. 27-33.

34 *DSA* i, p. 79.

35 Ibid., p. 85.

36 Ibid., p. 149.

37 Rodger, *The Safeguard of the Sea*, pp. 261-2.

38 *CSPS Eliz.iv*, 293.

39 J. L. Casado Soto, 'Atlantic Shipping in Sixteenth-Century Spain and the 1588 Armada', and Hugo O'Donnell, 'The Army of Flanders and the Invasion of England 1586-8', in Rodríguez-Salgado and Adams (eds.), *England, Spain and the Gran Armada*, pp. 95-133 and 216-35.

40 *CSPS Eliz. iv*, 301.

41 Ibid., 310.

42 Ibid., 318.

43 *DSA* i, pp. 5-6.

44 *CSPS Eliz. iv*, 321.

45 Ibid., 326.

46 Naish, 'Documents', p. 64.

47 *CSPS Eliz. iv*, 332.

48 Ibid., 334.

49 *DSA* i, p. 361.

6 Battle : The Channel and the Northern Seas, 23 July-3 September

1 The most accessible Spanish accounts of the campaign translated into English are the 'Diary of the Expedition to England sent by the Duke of Medina Sidonia to the King', *CSPS Eliz. iv, 402* and the 'Statement made by the Purser Pedro Coco Calderón', ibid., 439. See also ibid., 383, 384, 391, 397, 400, 416, 424. For accounts written from the English side, see *DSI* i and ii, *passim*, especially ii, pp. 1-18. Among modern accounts, Martin and Parker, *The Spanish Armada,* Rodger, *The Safeguard of the Sea* and Rodríguez-Salgado (ed.), *Armada,* are fundamental. For the fullest analysis of Philip's strategy, Parker, *Grand Strategy,* The most important modern Spanish writing is summarised in the essays in Rodríguez-Salgado and Adams (eds.), *England, Spain and the Gran Armada.*

2 *DSA i, pp. 6-7.*

3 Ibid.

4 Ibid., p. 9.

5 On Drake's role in the campaign, Cummins, *Drake,* pp. 305-40.

6 *CSPS Eliz iv.,* 360

7 Ibid., 439 (pp.441-2)

8 *DSA* i, pp. 12-13.

9 *CSPS Eliz iv,* 439 (p. 443)

10 Ibid.

11 Parker, *Grand Strategy,* pp. 229-50.

12 *CSPS Eliz. iv,* 402, pp. 397-8 and 439, pp. 443-4.

13 Cummins, *Drake,* 333-6.

14 *CSPS Eliz. iv,* 377, 391, 402, p. 401, 439, p.444.

15 Gracia Rivas, *La Sanidad en la Jornada de Inglaterra,* p. 290.

16 Thompson, 'Spanish Armada Guns', in *War and Society in Habsburg Spain,* p. 370.

17 *DSA ii, pp. 340-2.*

18 Ibid., ii, pp. 96-7.

19 *CSPS Eliz. iv,* 439, p. 447.

20 Flanagan, *Irish Wrecks*; Gracia Rivas, *La Sanidad en la Jornada de Inglaterra,* pp. 297-304; Cerezo Martínez, *Las Armadas de Felipe II,* pp. 372-5.

21 Martin and Parker, *Spanish Armada,* pp. 227-50.

22 Philip II to Catalina Micaela, Escorial, 19 Aug. 1588, printed by Bouza, *Cartas de Felipe II a sus hijas,* p. 158.

23 Vázquez de Leca to Philip II, San Lorenzo, 21 Aug., BL. Add. 28,263, f. 481.

24 *Consultas [Cntas]* Council of War, 7 and 19 Aug. 1588, AGS GA 235, ff. 71, 89; Idiáquez to Parma, 31 Aug. 1588, in L. P. Gachard, Correspondance de Philippe II sur les affaires des Pays-Bas (5 vols., Brussels, 1848-79), II, p. 841.

25 Gracia Rivas, *La Sanidad en la Jornada de Inglaterra*, pp. 307-20.

26 Martin and Parker, *Spanish Armada*, pp. 265, 267-8; Thompson, 'The Invincible Armada', p. 17.

27 *CSPV* viii, 735, 754, 780; A. W. Lovett, 'The vote of the *Millones* (1590), *Historical Journal*, xxx (1987), pp. 1-20.

28 Garrisson, *Sixteenth-Century France*, pp.380-2.

7 *After the Armada: Stalemate*

1 *CSPS Eliz. iv*, 662.

2 *Cntas*. War, 13 Dec. 1588 and 2 Feb. 1589, AGS GA 614, ff. 145 and 167.

3 Thompson, *War and Government*, pp. 156-8; Goodman, *Spanish Naval Power*, p. 156.

4 Lovett, 'The vote of the Millones', p. 465.

5 Morineau, *Incroyables gazettes*, pp. 345.

6 Wernham, *After the Armada*, pp. 234-6; Rodger, *The Safeguard of the Sea*, pp. 272-4.

7 *CSPV*, viii, 883, 903; K. R.Andrews, *Elizabethan Privateering, passim*; PRO SP 94/1v, ff. 96-9 and 99/1, f. 172.

8 Earle, *The Last Fight of the Revenge*, especially pp. 128-48; Rodger, *The Safeguard of the Sea*, pp. 279-80.

9 Parker, *Dutch Revolt*, p. 168.

10 Buisseret, *Henry IV*, p. 33.

11 Wernham, *After the Armada*, p. 235.

12 Rodger, *The Safeguard of the Sea*, pp. 274-5.

13 Van der Essen, *Farnese*, iv, p. 260.

14 Morineau, *Incroyables gazettes*, appendix II; Thompson, *War and Governmenti*, p. 16.

15 J. M. Carramolino, *Historia de Ávila*, iii, (Madrid, 1873), p. 45; R. L. Kagan, *Lucrecia's Dreams. Politics and Prophecy in Sixteenth-Century Spain*, (Los Angeles : 1990),p. 156.

16 Cummins, *Drake*, pp. 190-206; Rodger, *The Safeguard of the Sea*, p. 283.

17 *CSPV* ix, 437.

18 Wernham, *After the Armada*, pp. 156-97; Morineau, *Incroyables gazettes*, p. 46.

19 *CSPS* xiii, 256, 258, 259, 305.

20 *Cnta* Council of State 17 Dec. 1596, AGS E 114, no fol.

21 Thompson, *War and Government* p. 117.

22 *CSPS* xiii, 156-9; Wernham, *After the Armada*, p. 167.

23 CSPS, xiii, 203.

Conclusion

1 Boxer, *Portuguese Seaborne Empire*, p. vii. For a modern assessment of the campaign, Parker, *Grand Strategy*, pp. 281-96.

2 Rodger, *The Safeguard of the Sea*, p. 254.

3 On this, see Stradling, *Armada of Flanders*.

4 *Cntas* of Council of State, 27 May and 30 June 1614, AGS E 2028, no fols.

Bibliography

A note on published sources

The four-hundredth anniversary of the Armada in 1988 occasioned a number of important publications. Most notable of all was the commencement of the enormous task of publishing all relevant Spanish documentation on the Armada and its antecedents, from 1568; three volumes have thus far been published by Jorge Calvar Gross and his colleagues, taking the story to February 1588, in *La Batalla del Mar Océano [BMO]* The most important Spanish documentation not yet included in this magnificent collection is printed by C. Fernández Duro, *La Armada Invencible [AI]* and E. Herrera Oria, *La Armada Invencible [HO]*

English translations of several important documents are most readily available in G.P.B. Naish, 'Documents Illustrating the History of the Spanish Armada' in D.W. Waters, *The Elizabethan Navy and the Armada of Spain* and in N.A. Rodger, *The Armada in the Public Records*. Two classic volumes of documents have been reprinted by The Navy Records Society – J.S. Corbett, (ed.), *Papers Relating to the Navy during the Spanish War 1585-1587 [SW]* and John Knox Laughton (ed.), *State Papers relating to the defeat of the Spanish Armada, Anno 1588*, 2 vols., *[DSA]*. The various *Calendars of State Papers* remain of fundamental importance, although some errors are corrected in the *BMO;* most important is the *Calendar of State Papers… in …Simancas*, vol. iv, *Elizabeth 1587-1603 [CSPS Eliz. iv]*.

Spanish scholars published a number of major monographs to mark the anniversary; see the works of Casado Soto, Cerezo Martínez, O'Donnell y Duque de Estrada, Gómez-Centurión, Olesa Munido, Riano Lozano. Some important essays by these authors are published in the collections by Rodríguez-Salgado and Adams, *England, Spain and the Gran Armada* and Gallagher and Cruickshank, *God's Obvious Design*. Modern scholarship on the Armada is best (and most fully) represented in the exceptional study by Martin and Parker, *The Spanish Armada*, which supersedes all previous studies on the subject: see the second edition, 1999.

Adams, S., 'The Battle that never was: the Downs and the Armada Campaign', in Rodríguez-Salgado and Adams, *England, Spain and the Gran Armada*, pp. 45-69

Adams, S., 'The outbreak of the Elizabethan naval war against the Spanish Empire: The embargo of May 1585 and Sir Francis Drake's West India voyage', in M.J. Rodríguez-Salgado and S. Adams (eds.), *England, Spain and the Gran Armada, 1585-1604* (Edinburgh, 1991), pp. 45-69

Andrews, K.R., *Elizabethan Privateering: English privateering during the Spanish War, 1585-1603* (Cambridge, 1964)

Bakewell, P., *A History of Latin America. Empires and Sequels 1450-1930* (Oxford, 1997)

Bouza, F. (ed.), *Cartas de Felipe II a sus hijas* (Madrid, 1998)

Boxer, C.R., *The Portuguese Seaborne Empire 1415-1825* (Pelican Books, 1973)

Boyden, J.M., *The Courtier and the King. Ruy Gómez de Silva, Philip II and the Court of Spain* (Berkeley, 1995)

Braudel, F., *The Mediterranean and the Mediterranean World in the Age of Philip II* (2 vols., London, 1973)

Calendar of State Papers, Elizabeth, vols XIX-XXII (London, 1916-36)

Calendar of State Papers Relating to English Affairs Existing in...Venice, vol. VIII (London, 1894)

Calendar of State Papers Relating to English Affairs Preserved...in the Archives of Simancas, Elizabeth I-IV (London, 1892-9)

Calvar Gross, J., González-Allier Hierro, J.I., Duenas Fontán, M. and Mérida Valverde, M. del C., *La Batalla del Mar Océano*, 3 vols. (1568-88) (Madrid, 1988-93)

Casado Soto, J.L., 'Atlantic shipping in Sixteenth-Century Spain and the 1588 Armada', in Rodríguez-Salgado and Adams, *England, Spain and the Gran Armada*, pp. 95-132

Casado Soto, J.L., *Los Barcos Espanoles del Siglo XVI y la Gran Armada de 1588* (Madrid, 1988)

Cerezo Martínez, R., *Las Armadas de Felipe II* (Madrid, 1988)

Chaunu, P. and H., *Séville et l'Atlantique (1504-1650)* (Paris, 1955-9)

Checa, F., *Felipe II [Mecenas de las artes]* (Madrid, 1997)

Corbett, J.S. (ed.), *Papers relating to the Navy during The Spanish War 1585-1587* (reprint, Aldershot, 1987)

Croft, P., 'English commerce with Spain and the Armada War, 1558-1603', in Rodríguez-Salgado and Adams, *England, Spain and the Gran Armada*, pp. 236-63

Cummins, J., *Francis Drake* (London, 1997)

Earle, P., *The Last Fight of the Revenge* (London, 1992)

Essen, L. van der, *Alexandre Farnèse, prince de Parme, gouverneur-général des Pays-Bas (1545-92)*, (5 vols., Brussels, 1933-7)

Fernández-Armesto, F., *The Spanish Armada: The Experience of War* (Oxford, 1988)

Fernández Duro, C., *La Armada Invencible*, 2 vols. (Madrid, 1884-5)

Fernández Duro, C., *La conquista de las Azores en 1583* (Madrid, 1866)

Flanagan, L., *Irish Wrecks of the Spanish Armada* (Dublin, 1995)

Gallagher, P. and Cruickshank, D.W., *God's Obvious Design: Papers for the Spanish Armada Sympolsium, Sligo, 1988* (London, 1990)

Garrisson, J., *A History of Sixteenth-Century France, 1483-1598* (Basingstoke, 1995)

Glete, J., *Warfare at Sea, 1500-1650. [Maritime Conflicts and the Transformation of Europe]* (London, 2000)

Gómez-Centurión, C., *Felipe II, la Empresa de Inglaterra y el Comercio Septentrional (1566-1609) (Madrid, 1998)*

Gómez-Centurión, C., *La Invencible y le Empresa de Inglaterra* (Madrid, 1988)

Goodman, D., *Spanish Naval Power, 1589-1665: Reconstruction and Defeat* (Cambridge, 1997)

Gracia Rivas, M., *La Sanidad en la Jornada de Inglaterra, 1587-8* (Madrid, 1988)

Gracia Rivas, M., *Los Tercios en la Gran Armada, 1587-8* (Madrid, 1989)

Gracia Rivas, M., 'The medical services of the Gran Armada', in Rodríguez-Salgado and Adams (eds.), *England, Spain and the Gran Armada'*, pp.197-215.

Green, J.M., "I My Self': Queen Elizabeth's oration at Tilbury camp', *Sixteenth Century Journal*, XXVIII (1997), pp. 421-45.

Guilmartin, J.F., *Gunpowder and Galleys: changing technology and Mediterranean warfare in the sixteenth century* (Cambridge, 1974)

Guy, J., *Tudor England* (Oxford, 1988)

Hakluyt, R., *The Principal Navigations Voyages Traffiques & Discoveries of the English Nation* (1599-1600, reprinted, Glasgow, 1903-05)

Herrera Oria, E., *Felipe II y el Marqués de Santa Cruz en la Empresa de Inglaterra* (Madrid, 1946)

Herrera Oria, E., *La Armada Invencible* (Valladolid, 1929)

Hoffman, P.E., *The Spanish Crown and the Defence of the Caribbean, 1535-1585: Precedent, Patrimonialism and Royal Parsimony* (Baton Rouge, 1985)

Kamen, H., *Philip of Spain* (New Haven, 1997)

Kelsey, H., *Sir Francis Drake, the Queen's Pirate* (London and New Haven, 1998)

Kennedy, P.M. *The Rise and Fall of British Naval Mastery* (London, 1976)

Kenny, R.W., *Elizabeth's Admiral: the political career of Charles Howard earl of Nottingham 1536-1624* (Baltimore, 1970)

Kossman, E.H. and Mellink, A.F., *Texts Concerning the Revolt of the Netherlands* (Cambridge, 1974)

Laughton, J.K., *State Papers Relating to the Defeat of the Spanish Armada, Anno 1588*, (London, 1895, reprinted 1989)

Lewis, M., *The Hawkins Dynasty: Three Generations of a Tudor Family* (London, 1969)

Loades, D.M., *Mary Tudor: a life* (Oxford, 1995)

Loades, D.M., *The Tudor Navy: an administrative, political and military history* (Aldershot, 1992)

Lovett, A.W., *Early Habsburg Spain 1517-1598* (Oxford, 1986)

Lovett, A.W., *Philip II and Mateo Vázquez de Leca : The Government of Spain (1572-1592)* (Geneva, 1977)

Lyon, E., *The Enterprise of Florida: Pedro Menéndez de Avilés and the Spanish Conquest of 1565-8* (Gainesville, 1976)

MacCaffrey, W.T., *Elizabeth I (London, New York, 1993)*

Martin, C., *Full Fathoms Five: Wrecks of the Spanish Armada* (London, 1975)

Martin C., and Parker, G., *The Spanish Armada* (Manchester University Press, 1999)

Martin, P., *Spanish Armada Prisoners: The Story of the Nuestra Senora del Rosario and her crew, and of other prisoners in England 1587-97* (Exeter, 1988)

Mattingly, G., *The Defeat of the Spanish Armada* (London, 1959)

Morineau, M., *Incroyables gazettes et fabuleux métaux: les retours des trésor américains d'après les gazettes hollandaises (XVIe-XVIIIe siècles)* (Paris and Cambridge, 1985)

O'Donnell y Duque de Estrada, H., *La fuerza de desembarco de la Gran Armada contra Inglaterra 1588* (Madrid, 1989)

O'Donnell y Duque de Estrada, H., 'The Army of Flanders and the Invasion of England 1586-8', in Rodríguez-Salgado and Adams, *England, Spain and the Gran Armada*, pp. 216-35

O'Donnell y Duque de Estrada, H., 'The Requirements of the Duke of Parma for the Conquest of England', in Gallagher and Cruickshank, *God's Obvious Design*, pp. 85-99

Olesa Munido, F.F., *La organización naval de los estados Mediterráneos y en especial de Espana durante los siglos XVI y XVII*, 2 vols. (Madrid, 1968)

Parente, G., et alii, *Los sucesos de Flandes de 1588 en relación con la empresa de Inglaterra* (Madrid, 1988)

Parker, G., 'If the Armada had landed', *History* LXI (1976), pp. 358-68

Parker, G., 'The Dreadnought revolution of Tudor England', *Mariner's Mirror*, LXXXII (1996), pp. 269-300

Parker, G., *The Grand Strategy of Philip II* (London and New Haven, 1988)

Pi Corrales, M. de P., *La Otra Invencible, 1574: Espana y las potencias nórdicas* (Madrid, 1983)

Pierson, P., *Commander of the Armada: The seventh duke of Medina Sidonia* (London and New Haven, 1989)

Riano Lozano, F., *Los medios navales de Alejandro Farnesio 1587-1588* (Madrid, 1989)

Rodger, N.A.M., *The Safeguard of the Sea. A Naval History of Britain, I, 660-1649* (London, 1997)

Rodríguez-Salgado, M.J., *Armada*, (London, 1988)

Rodriguez-Salgado, M.J., *The Changing Face of Empire: Charles V, Philip II and Habsburg Authority, 1551-9* (Cambridge, 1988)

Rodríguez-Salgado, M.J., and Adams, S. (eds.), *England, Spain and the Gran Armada, 1585-1604* (Edinburgh, 1991)

Smith, A.G.R., *The Emergence of a Nation State. The commonwealth of England 1529-1660* (London, 1997)

Sténuit, R., *Treasures of the Armada* (Newton Abbot, 1972)

Stradling, R.A., *The Armada of Flanders: Spanish Maritime Policy and European War, 1568-1668* (Cambridge, 1992)

Strong, R., *The Cult of Elizabeth. Elizabethan Portraiture and Pageantry* (London, 1999)

Thompson, I.A.A., 'Spanish Armada Guns', *Mariner's Mirror*, LXI (1976), pp. 355-71

Thompson, I.A.A., 'The Appointment of the Duke of Medina Sidonia to the Command of the Spanish Armada', *Historical Journal* XII (1969), pp. 197-216

Thompson, I.A.A., 'The Armada and Administrative Reform: The Spanish Council of War in the Reign of Philip II', *English Historical Review* LXXXII (1967), pp. 698-725

Thompson, I.A.A., 'The Invincible Armada', in *War and Society in Habsburg Spain. Selected Essays*, (Aldershot, 1992)

Thompson, I.A.A., *War and Government in Habsburg Spain 1560-1620* (London, 1976)

Waters, D.W., *The Elizabethan Navy and the Armada of Spain* (Greenwich, 1975)

Wernham, R.B., *After the Armada: Elizbethan England and the struggle for western Europe, 1588-95* (Oxford, 1984)

Wernham, R.B., *Before the Armada: the growth of English foreign policy, 1485-1588* (London, 1966)

Wernham, R.B., *The Expedition of Sir John Norris and Sir Francis Drake to Spain and Portugal, 1589*, Navy Records Society CXXVII (London, 1988)

Wernham, R.B., *The Return of the Armadas: The Last Years of the Elizabethan War against Spain, 1595-1603* (Oxford, 1994)

Williams, N., *The Sea Dogs. Privateers, Plunder and Piracy in the Elizabethan Age* (London, 1975)

Appendix I

The Armada at Lisbon, 9 May 1588

	Tons	Soldiers	Sailors	Artillery
SQUADRON OF PORTUGAL (Duke of Medina Sidonia)				
San Martín (flagship)	1000	300	177	48
San Juan (vice flagship)	1050	321	179	50
San Márcos	790	292	117	33
San Felipe	800	415	117	40
San Luis	830	376	116	38
San Mateo	750	277	120	34
Santiago	520	300	93	24
Florencia	961	400	86	52
San Cristóbal	352	300	78	20
San Bernardo	352	250	81	21
Agusta	166	55	57	13
Julia	166	44	72	14
SQUADRON OF VIZCAYA (Juan Martinez de Recalde)				
Santa Ana (flagship)	768	323	114	30
Gran Grin (vice flagship)	1160	256	73	28
Santiago	666	214	102	25
Concepción de Zubelzu	468	90	70	16
Concepción de Juanes Delcano	418	164	61	18
La Magdalena	530	193	67	18
San Juan	350	114	80	21
La Maria Juan	665	172	100	24
La Manuela	520	125	54	12
Sta Maria de Montemayor	707	206	45	18
Maria de Aguirre	70	20	23	6
Isabella	71	20	24	10
Miguel Suso	96	20	26	6
San Esteban	78	20	26	6

	Tons	Soldiers	Sailors	Artillery
SQUADRON OF GALLEONS OF CASTILE (Diego Flores de Valdes)				
San Cristóbal (flagship)	700	205	120	36
San Juan Bautista (vice flagship)	750	207	136	24
San Pedro	530	141	131	24
San Juan	530	163	113	24
Santiago el Mayor	530	210	132	24
San Felipe y Santiago	530	151	116	24
La Asunción	530	199	114	24
Nuestra Senora del Barrio	530	155	108	24
Sant Medel y Celedón	530	160	101	24
Santa Ana	250	91	80	24
Nuestra Senora de Begoña	750	174	123	24
La Trinidad	872	180	122	24
Santa Catalina	882	190	159	24
San Juan Bautista	652	192	93	24
Nuestra Señora del Rosario (patache)	75	20	25	24
San Antonio de Padua	75	20	46	12
SQUADRON OF ANDALUSIA (Pedro de Valdes)				
Nuestra Senora del Rosario (flagship)	1150	304	118	46
San Francisco (vice flagship)	915	222	56	21
San Juan Bautista	810	245	89	31
San Juan de Gargarin	569	165	56	16
La Concepción	862	185	71	20
Duquesa Santa Ana	900	280	77	23
Santa Catalina	730	231	77	23
La Trinidad	650	192	74	13
San Maria del Juncal	730	228	80	20
San Bartolome	976	240	72	27
Espíritu Santo	70	31	33	43
SQUADRON OF GUIPUZCOA (Miguel de Oquendo)				
Santa Ana (flagship)	1200	303	82	47
Nuestra Señora de la Rosa (viceflagship)	945	225	64	26

	Tons	Soldiers	Sailors	Artillery
San Salvador	958	321	75	25
San Estéban	936	196	68	26
Santa Marta	548	173	63	20
Santa Bárbara	525	154	45	12
San Buenaventura	379	168	53	21
Maria San Juan	291	110	30	12
Santa Cruz	680	138	36	18
Doncella	500	156	32	16
La Asunción	60	20	16	9
San Bernabé	69	20	23	9
Nuestra Senora de Guadalupe	50	0	15	1
La Madalena	50	0	14	1

SQUADRON OF THE LEVANT
(Martin de Bertendona)

	Tons	Soldiers	Sailors	Artillery
La Regazona (flagship)	1294	344	80	30
La Lavia (vice flagship)	728	203	71	25
La Rata Santa Maria Encoronada	820	335	84	35
San Juan de Sicilia	800	279	63	26
La Trinidad Valencera	1100	281	79	42
La Anunciada	703	196	79	24
Sant Nicolas Prodaneli	834	274	81	26
La Juliana	860	325	70	32
Santa María de Visón	666	236	71	18
La Trinidad de Scala	900	307	79	22

SQUADRON OF HULKS
(Juan López de Medina)

	Tons	Soldiers	Sailors	Artillery
El Gran Grifon (flagship)	650	243	43	38
Sant Salvador (vice flagship)	650	218	43	24
Perro Marino	200	70	24	7
Falcon Blanco Mayor	500	161	36	16
Castillo Negro	750	239	34	27
Barca de Amburg	600	239	34	23
Casa de Paz Grande	600	198	27	26
San Pedro Mayor	213	213	28	29
El Sanson	500	200	31	18
San Pedro Menor	500	157	23	18

	Tons	Soldiers	Sailors	Artillery
Barca de Anzique	450	200	25	26
Falcon Blanco Mediano	300	76	27	16
San Andres	400	150	28	14
Casa de Paz Chica	350	162	24	15
Ciervo Volante	400	200	22	18
Paloma Blanca	250	56	20	12
La Ventura	160	58	14	4
Santa Bárbara	370	70	22	10
Santiago	600	56	30	19
David	450	50	24	7
El Gato	400	40	22	9
San Gabriel	280	35	20	4
Esayas	280	30	16	4

PATACHES AND ZABRAS
(Antonio Hurtado de Mendoza)

	Tons	Soldiers	Sailors	Artillery
Nuestra Senora del Pilar de Zaragoza (flagship)	300	109	51	11
La Caridad (English)	180	70	36	12
Sanct Andrés (Scottish)	150	40	29	12
El Crucifijo	150	40	29	8
Nuestra Señora del Puerto	55	30	33	8
La Concepción de Carasa	70	30	42	5
Nuestra Senora de Begona	64	20	26	5
La Concepcion de Capetillo	60	20	31	10
San Jerónimo	55	20	37	4
Nuestra Señora de Gracia	57	20	34	5
La Concepción de Francisco de Lastero	75	20	29	6
Nuestra Señora de Guadalupe	70	20	42	6
San Francisco	70	37	57	6
La Concepción de Castro	70	20	27	2
Espíritu Santo	75	20	27	2
Nuestra Señora de Fresneda	70	20	27	2
La Trinidad	75	23	23	2
Nuestra Señora de Castro	75	26	26	2
San Andrés	75	15	15	2
La Concepción de Somanilla	75	31	31	2
Sancta Catalina	75	23	23	2
Sant Juan de Carassa	75	23	23	2
La Asunción	75	23	23	2

	Tons	Soldiers	Sailors	Artillery
THE GALLEASSES OF NAPLES (Don Hugo de Moncada)				
San Lorenzo (flagship)	600	262	124	50
Patrona	600	178	112	50
Girona	600	169	120	50
Napolitana	600	264	112	50
THE GALLEYS OF PORTUGAL (Diego de Medrano)				
(Unnamed flagship)		106	5	
Princesa		90	5	
Diana		94	5	
Bázana		72	5	
TOTALS	61627	19506	8221	2537

In addition, the Galleasses of Naples carried 1200 oarsmen and the Galleys of Portugal carried 888

Source : Herrera Oria, *La Armada Invencible*, pp. 384-405. These figures correct errors in the original calculations. The official figures are given in the text (p.118).

For a more detailed analysis, see Martin and Parker, *Spanish Armada*, pp. 261-5.

Appendix II

The English ships in the campaign

	Tonnage	Sailors	Gunners	Soldiers	Total
ROYAL SHIPS					
Ark Royal	800	270	34	126	425
Elizabeth Bonaventura	600	150	24	76	250
Rainbow	500	150	24	76	250
Golden Lion	500	150	24	76	250
White Bear	1,000	300	40	150	500
Vanguard	500	150	24	76	250
Revenge	500	150	24	76	250
Elizabeth Jonas	900	300	40	150	500
Victory	800	270	34	126	400
Antelope	400	120	20	30	160
Triumph	1,100	300	40	160	500
Dreadnought	400	130	20	40	200
Mary Rose	600	150	24	76	250
Nonpareil	500	150	24	76	250
Hope	600	160	25	85	250
Galley Bonavolia	—	—	—	—	250
Swiftsure	400	120	20	40	180
Swallow	360	110	20	30	160
Foresight	300	110	20	20	160
Aid	250	90	16	14	120
Bull	200	80	12	8	100
Tiger	200	80	12	8	100
Tramontana	150	55	8	7	70
Scout	120	55	8	7	60
Achates	100	45	8	7	60
Charles	70	36	4	—	45
Moon	60	34	4	—	40
Advice	50	31	4	—	40
Merlin	50	20	4	—	35
Spy	50	31	4	—	40
Sun	40	26	5	—	30
Cygnet	30	—	—	—	20

	Tonnage	Sailors	Gunners	Soldiers	Total
Brigandine	90	—	—	—	35
George Hoy	100	16	4	—	24

MERCHANT SHIPS UNDER FRANCIS DRAKE

	Tonnage				Total
Galleon Leicester	400				160
Merchant Royal	400				160
Edward Bonaventure	300				120
Roebuck	300				120
Golden Noble	250				110
Griffin	200				100
Minion	200				80
Bark Talbot	200				90
Thomas Drake	200				80
Spark	200				90
Hopewell	200				100
Galleon Dudley	250				96
Virgin God Save Her	200				70
Hope Hawkyns	200				80
Bark Bond	150				70
Bark Bonner	150				70
Bark Hawkyns	150				70
Unity	80				40
Elizabeth Drake	60				30
Bark Buggins	80				50
Elizabeth Founes	80				50
Bark St Leger	160				80
Bark Manington	160				80
Hearts-ease	—-				24
Golden Hinde	50				30
Makeshift	60				40
Diamond of Dartmouth	60				40
Speedwell	60				14
Best Yonge	140				70
Chance	60				40
Delight	50				40
Nightingale	40				30
Unnamed caravel	30				20
Flyboat Yonge	50				50

	Tonnage	Sailors	Gunners	Soldiers	Total

SHIPS PAID FOR BY THE CITY OF LONDON

	Tonnage	Sailors	Gunners	Soldiers	Total
Hercules	300				120
Toby	250				100
Mayflower	200				90
Minion	200				90
Royal Defence	160				80
Ascension	200				200
Gift of God	180				80
Primrose	200				90
Margaret and John	200				90
Golden Lion	140				70
Diana	80				40
Bark Burr	160				70
Tiger	200				90
Brave	160				70
Red Lion	200				90
Centurion	250				100
Passport	80				40
Moonshine	60				30
Thomas Bonaventure	140				70
Release	60				30
George Noble	120				80
Anthony	100				60
Toby	120				70
Salamander	110				60
Rose Lion	100				50
Antelope	120				60
Jewel	110				60
Pansy	100				70
Prudence	120				60
Dolphin	110				70

MERCHANT SHIPS PAID FOR BY THE CROWN

	Tonnage	Sailors	Gunners	Soldiers	Total
Susan Parnell	220				80
Violet	220				60
Solomon	170				80

	Tonnage	Sailors	Gunners	Soldiers	Total
Anne Frances	180				70
George Bonaventura	200				80
Jane Bonaventura	100				50
Vineyard	160				60
Samuel	140				50
White Lion	140				50
Disdain	80				45
Lark	50				20
Edward of Maldon	186				30
Marigold	30				12
Black Dog	20				10
Katharine	20				10
Fancy	50				20
Pippin	20				8
Nightingale	160				16
	24,166				11,679

In addition, a further eighty-one coasters and victuallers carried about 5000 men, bringing the total number of men who served in the campaign to about 16,000.

Based upon *DSA*, ii, pp. 323-331.

Index

Numbers in bold denote an illustration